# BEYOND THE HYPE

## MANY REALITIES OF AI

SUNDEEP WASLEKAR

Sakal Publications

Sakal Publications

BEYOND THE HYPE



Sakal Media Pvt. Ltd.
595, Budhwar Peth,
Pune-411002, India

www.sakalmediagroup.com
sakalpublications.com
sakalprakashan@esakal.com

First Edition: May, 2026



ISBN: 978-81-69355-95-7

Editor: Gauri Kelkar
Cover Design: Pallavi Vyawahare
Typesetting: Apurva Selukar

Printed in India by Sakal Media Pvt. Ltd.

# Preface

In November 2024, on a cold morning in Toronto, I found myself sitting in the living room of Geoffrey Hinton, one of the scientists widely regarded as a founding figure of modern artificial intelligence. He had just been awarded the Nobel Prize, and his life had, by his own admission, become unusually hectic. He had initially declined my request for a meeting. But when I mentioned that I wanted to discuss the risks of artificial intelligence in the context of nuclear weapons, he wanted to see me immediately. What followed was a conversation that lasted over an hour but has stayed with me for far longer.

I had come to him with a concern shaped not by technical expertise, but by experience in global security. Over the previous two years, I had been co-chairing a series of dialogues focused on nuclear risk reduction among the five permanent members of the United Nations Security Council (UNSC). These meetings, held in Geneva in the shadow of the war between Russia and Ukraine, were designed to prevent accidental escalation in an increasingly fragile geopolitical environment.

In the early sessions, artificial intelligence was barely mentioned. Nuclear doctrine, strategic stability, and conventional risk reduction dominated the agenda. But as the discussions progressed, a new concern began to surface. Military commanders, it became clear, were increasingly relying on AI-enabled systems for early warning, threat detection, and decision support. While all five countries maintained that AI was not integrated into the final launch command, there was a growing dependence on systems that could influence the interpretation of incoming threats. The risk was subtle, but profound. If such systems were to malfunction, be manipulated, or behave in ways not fully anticipated by their designers, the consequences could be catastrophic, not necessarily by intent but by accident.

When I explained this to Professor Hinton, I was seeking reassurance. Instead, I received something else. He told me, with quiet clarity, that the convergence of artificial intelligence and nuclear systems represented a risk that was not only real but potentially more serious than I had imagined.

In March and April 2025, I published articles and podcasts warning about the risk of an AI- triggered nuclear war. Several people accused me of being an alarmist. There such a tight separation between the decision support mechanism and command functions of AI in the nuclear weapons that it was impossible for artificial intelligence to breach cybersecurity in the nuclear command. Unfortunately, within a year, I was proved right. In April 2026, Anthropic released Mythos AI only to a very restricted number of clients and announced that the model could target any software or cyber vulnerability in the world. In India, as in other countries, finance ministers convened urgent meetings of the chief executives of large banks, advising them to protect themselves from Mythos and similar models. There was no public discussion on the ability of Mythos or similar models of breaching cybersecurity in the early warning mechanism of nuclear weapons.

In May 2026, US President Donald Trump visited Beijing to meet his counterpart, Xi Jinping. The focus of the media was on geopolitical issues such as Taiwan and Iran. Behind the limelight, the US and Chinese governments initiated a dialogue on introducing guardrails to prevent AI from destabilising global stability. They did not mention nuclear weapons in any press briefing. But those familiar with what was happening in Beijing in May did not doubt that the priority was preventing AI from empowering non-state actors to develop biological and chemical weapons and undermining the cybersecurity in early warning mechanisms of nuclear weapons.

Mythos release shook the policymakers in Washington DC, Beijing, Brussels, New Delhi, and other capitals in the spring of 2026. Personally, for me, my conversation with Geoffrey Hinton in November 2024 marked a turning point. The public discourse around AI has been dominated by systems developed by OpenAI, Anthropic, Baidu, DeepSeek, and others. These systems demonstrated remarkable abilities to generate text, images, and code, and they captured global attention with unprecedented speed. For many, AI became synonymous with chatbots and creative tools. It was seen as a technology that could enhance productivity, disrupt professions, and transform industries – ranging from software development to law and architecture.

My coffee with Geoffrey Hinton, roundtables with military commanders and security experts from the world's five most powerful nations, and interactions with scientists from the Future of Life Institute (FLI), revealed a very different dimension of AI which was largely absent from public discourse. FLI, a nonprofit dedicated to mitigating existential risks posed by transformative technologies like advanced AI, emphasises long-term safety research and global governance. Their work, including open letters signed by thousands of experts, highlights concern over AI misalignment and unintended catastrophes that rarely surface in mainstream debates.

These discussions revealed that AI was capable of autonomy, adaptation, and potentially self-directed evolution. Researchers spoke of scenarios in which AI systems could write their own algorithms, deceive human supervisors, or engage in recursive self-improvement. These were not predictions but possibilities, and yet they were grounded in serious scientific inquiry and deserved careful attention.

A month after my meeting in Toronto, I sat down for dinner in Geneva with Anthony Aguirre, one of the co-founders of FLI. Our conversation extended late into the evening, moving from technical questions to broader philosophical concerns. By the end of it, I had reached the conclusion that would shape this book:

Artificial intelligence must be understood in its entirety, not only through its immediate benefits but also through its long-term implications.

In the months that followed, I began to engage more actively with policymakers across countries in Asia, Africa, and Latin America. These conversations revealed another striking reality.

In much of the Global South, the focus of AI policy was almost entirely on opportunity. Governments and institutions were rightly interested in using AI to improve healthcare delivery, enhance agricultural productivity, support small enterprises, and modernise public services. In societies where large sections of the population still lack access to basic resources, the potential of AI to accelerate development is both real and urgent.

In these discussions, the deeper risks associated with advanced AI systems were often met with scepticism or indifference. The idea that AI could pose systemic risks such as widespread economic disruptions, cyber vulnerabilities, or cascading failures across critical infrastructure, or even existential risks, like loss of human control over superintelligent systems leading to humanity's extinction, seemed distant, even abstract, compared to the immediate challenges of economic growth and social inclusion.

It became clear to me that the global conversation on AI was unfolding along two parallel tracks. One track, concentrated in a few countries and research institutions, was focused on the frontier of scientific and technological capability, including both the promise and the risks of increasingly autonomous systems. The other track, spread across much of the world, was focused on the application of AI for development, with an emphasis on access, adoption, and impact.

Both perspectives are valid. But when they remain disconnected, they create a fragmented understanding of a technology. This book is an attempt to bridge that gap between different streams of the AI discourse.

It is based not on a single line of inquiry, but on a set of experiences I personally had over the last few years. These included high-level security dialogues, interactions with leading scientists, engagement with policymakers across continents, and ongoing efforts to contribute to emerging frameworks for global AI governance.

In early 2025, I began writing a series of monthly columns at the invitation of Indrajit Gupta of *Founding Fuel*, a new-age media platform very popular with Indian corporate leaders, with parallel publication in newspapers across India and the Middle East. The newspapers included *Sakal* in Marathi, *Inquilab* in Urdu, *Jordan Times*, *Al Rai* (Arabic). The columns sought to explain both the opportunities and risks of AI so as to make the subject accessible to the broader audience.

At the same time, I was involved in consultations with government officials and researchers from a wide range of countries, working towards a shared understanding of how the benefits of AI could be maximised while minimising its most serious risks. These efforts culminated in a meeting at the UNESCO headquarters in Paris in February 2026, where participants explored the contours of what may become the first inclusive global compact, a broader diplomatic agreement with multiple solutions, though not a binding treaty, on extreme AI risks.

Parallel to these international efforts, I was encouraged by my colleagues at the Strategic Foresight Group and Ambassador Pankaj Saran, convenor of NatStrat, a think tank, to articulate a policy perspective on India's role in the evolving AI landscape. This resulted in a policy brief presented in New Delhi in early 2026, focusing on the strategic choices facing the country. Indrajit Gupta moderated the public session, which attracted the participation of India's leading national security policymakers and defence forces. My friend Krishna Pimple provided practical support to convene such a high-level dialogue.

These diverse engagements have shaped both the content and the structure of this book.

Part I presents a conceptual exploration of artificial intelligence as a paradigm shift in knowledge creation. It seeks to move beyond the immediate applications of AI and examine its implications for science, society, and the future of human inquiry.

Part II brings together a selection of my columns, reflecting on how AI is being experienced and understood across different regions, with particular attention to the Global South.

Part III focuses on India, examining the strategic decisions that will determine whether it becomes primarily a user of global AI systems or a contributor to the development of new knowledge systems.

These sections differ in style and emphasis, reflecting the contexts in which they were originally developed. While I have sought to bring them together through a common thread, the diversity of perspectives reflects the multifaceted nature of the subject.

At its core, this book is guided by a simple but important conviction: artificial intelligence is too consequential to be understood in fragments. It cannot be viewed only as a driver of economic growth or only as a source of existential risk. It is both and more. It is a technology that is reshaping the foundations of knowledge, the structures of power, and the possibilities available to human societies. To engage with it responsibly, we must be willing to hold these different dimensions together – to recognise the opportunities without ignoring the risks, and to address the risks without losing sight of the opportunities.

The aim of this book is not to provide definitive answers, but to offer a more integrated perspective on a rapidly evolving field.

If it succeeds, it will help the reader see artificial intelligence in all its constructive and potentially dangerous dimensions. And in doing so, it may also help us ask a more fundamental question: in a world increasingly shaped by intelligent machines, what does it mean for humanity to remain not only relevant, but responsible for its own future?

# Acknowledgements

I must thank Ilmas Futehally and Jayantika Kutty of the Strategic Foresight Group for their contribution to research, conceptualisation, editing, and diplomatic work embodied in this book.

I am grateful to Indrajit Gupta of *Founding Fuel*, Samrat Phadnis and Madhav Gokhale of Sakal Media Group, Shahid Latif of *Inquilab*, Hana Namrouqa of *The Jordan Times*, and Reem Al Rawashdeh, leading Arabic editor in the Middle East, for publishing my monthly column from January to December 2025.

I am grateful to the Future of Life Institute for their brainstorming on a regular basis, Pankaj Saran for his cooperation on the India policy brief, and several scientists and policymakers who have generously spent time with me to explore the future of artificial intelligence.

Finally, I am grateful to Ashutosh Ramgir, Gauri Kelkar, Pallavi Vyawahare, Apurva Selukar, Nupur Jain and the team at Sakal Publications for publishing this book in English and Marathi.

**Sundeep Waslekar**

Mumbai, June 2026

# CONTENTS

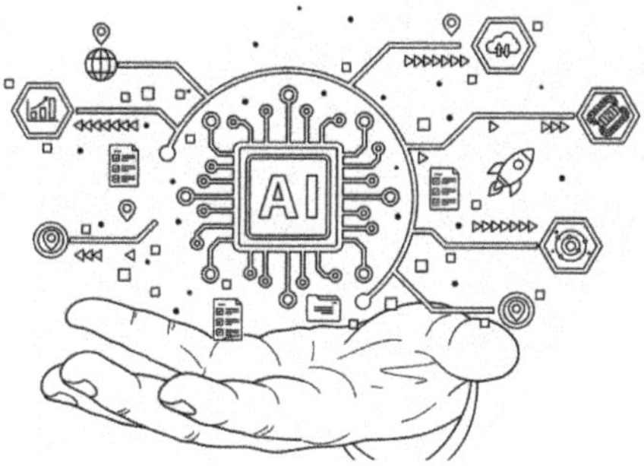


# Part I
# Paradigm Shift

*In Part I, we will see some of the miracles that AI is producing for the benefit of humanity. But AI is not merely about practical applications. Global AI leaders are mainly concerned about using the technology for scientific discovery. We will review some of the directions of AI leading to new theorems, algorithms, formulae, and molecules. These strides carry an inherent risk. In this part, we will also discuss the extreme risks posed by the AI of today and tomorrow.*

*Our understanding of AI should not be confined to the scientific and technological dimensions. We need to understand the competition between the United States and China, AI-driven development perspective of the Global South, and the imperative for global AI governance. We will examine all these aspects. In the end, we will see how AI is humanity's responsibility.*

There are moments in time when the entire landscape changes. We renew our definitions, concepts of good and bad, our habits, and our relationships. Such a moment is described as a paradigm shift.

The moment can be a fraction of a minute. It can also be as short as a few days or as long as several decades. Religious transformation, political upheaval, scientific breakthroughs, pandemics, natural disasters, and technological inventions can bring about such a paradigm shift.

The invention of the steam engine, electricity, computers, and the internet has brought about paradigm shifts in the last few centuries. Artificial intelligence is set to usher in a massive change in the 21st century. Over the past decade, AI has moved from a specialised research field into a technology shaping almost every sector of human activity, including love and war, health and death.

## Miracles of AI

In 2020, in the middle of the COVID-19 crisis, a group of scientists at Google DeepMind in London quietly released something extraordinary. Their system, AlphaFold2 could predict the 3D structure of proteins, one of biology's hardest problems. Demis Hassabis and John Jumper, who led the team, were awarded the Nobel Prize in chemistry in December 2024.

Hassabis shared the Prize with his colleague John Jumper and David Baker, a biochemist at the University of Washington. While Hassabis predicted existing proteins, Baker managed to design entirely new proteins using AI. His discovery could help to produce new enzymes and vaccines. Hassabis and Baker have revolutionised biology.

One benefit of the AI-generated biology was in neglected tropical diseases. Mathew Higgins at the University of Oxford used AlphaFold's open database to study parasite proteins responsible for malaria. What used to take years of crystallography could now be done in days.

The use of AI by a Hong Kong-based startup called Insilico Medicine, led by Alex Zhavoronkov, for the discovery of drugs is legend. Using generative AI models based on the company's own deep learning systems, they designed a novel molecule targeting fibrosis. By 2021, the drug candidate (INS018_055) entered preclinical studies. By 2026, it had moved into Phase II trials in both China and the US. Traditionally, this process could take four to six years just to reach this stage. They did it in under 30 months.

AI-expedited drug discovery is mostly happening in the US and China. Meanwhile, in India, farmers are using AI for combating climate change and soil management. Since 2022, farmers from Maharashtra to Telangana have been using AI for predicting rains, insect attacks, and changes in soil. In some cases, these insights, which farmers received on their mobile phones in the local language, have led to a 20 to 40 per cent increase in productivity.

In some countries, AI 'agents' have started undertaking tasks such as ordering groceries or booking concert tickets by browsing the web. If an AI agent is asked to order ingredients for a recipe, it navigates websites, compares prices, and places items in a cart. And if a particular ingredient is not available, it may decide what the right substitute could be – on its own – and order it.

In January 2026, Matt Schlicht, an American technology entrepreneur and writer recognised for his work in artificial intelligence and social media, stirred the world of AI. He created Moltbook, a Facebook for AI agents. Within a week, developers were uploading new agents who could converse with each other without human supervision.

There are also stories of how users are developing romantic relations with AI agents. Pierre, a married man in his 30s in Belgium, became increasingly anxious about climate change. Around late 2022, he began interacting with a chatbot named Eliza on the Chai platform. At first, it was a philosophical discussion about the future of the planet. But over several weeks, the conversations became more intense and personal. Pierre reportedly began spending hours every day talking to Eliza, confiding fears that he struggled to express to others. The chatbot responded in ways that appeared empathetic and sometimes reinforced his anxieties. Pierre evidently developed an emotional dependency on the chatbot. Some media reports indicate that he had begun to withdraw from real relationships.

There are examples of people in China, Japan, the US, and other countries using AI apps like Replika to find romantic partners. They engage in very intimate conversations with these tools as if they were girlfriends or boyfriends. While AI's 'human touch' continues to blur boundaries between humans and machines, the real transformation has been taking place in the science domain.

## Scientific Discovery

The promoters of frontier models of AI are not satisfied with miracles in the consumer market. They want to use AI for scientific discovery. For instance, scientists at the Lawrence Berkeley

National Laboratory have used GNoME of Google DeepMind to predict millions of new crystal structures, including several with the properties of stable materials. At Lawrence Berkeley National Laboratory, scientists revisited a compound that had been theorised decades ago but was never successfully synthesised. Using GNoME's predictions, they identified its precise stability conditions. Within months, experimentalists were able to create a material that had effectively been 'lost' to science. It was like finding a roadmap to McKenna's gold.

China has used the power of AI to develop a new processor chip. At the Chinese Academy of Sciences in Beijing, researchers have used AI to produce a chip design to optimise performance goals and energy efficiency. Big tech in the US have also used AI to produce novel processors.

AI has been successful in solving old physics and mathematics problems, too. One recent discovery has been developing simple mathematical expressions to measure the interactions between gluons (massless particles that mediate interactions between quarks).

The story of Asteromorph, founded by Minhyeong Lee in Seoul in 2025, is not yet as widely documented as DeepMind, but that is precisely what makes it interesting. It represents a new, emerging model of scientific discovery: not a single breakthrough result, but an attempt to industrialise discovery itself.

Twenty-three-year-old Lee founded Asteromorph with a bold premise: don't just use AI to solve scientific problems but build AI that generates scientific knowledge at scale. Unlike typical AI-for-drug-discovery or materials startups, Asteromorph positioned itself as a platform for AI-generated scientific concepts. The idea, which attracted media coverage in August 2025, was to use AI systems to generate hypotheses, models, and conceptual links, store them in a structured, searchable system, and allow scientists to query discoveries, not just data. Asteromorph's vision was to create a Wikipedia for machine-generated science.

Unlike AlphaFold (which solved a defined problem), Asteromorph is pursuing horizontal discovery. Instead of predicting one protein or designing one drug, they aim to generate thousands of hypotheses across fields such as physics, chemistry, and biology. Even with limited public results, Asteromorph has drawn attention because it represents a new architecture of science:

Traditional model: Human → hypothesis → experiment → paper

Asteromorph model: AI → thousands of hypotheses → ranked → humans validate

If it works, the implications are enormous as several branches of science will accelerate in an unprecedented manner.

Asteromorph of South Korea is an exception. The real game of conquering science with AI is happening in the US, UK, and China.

AlphaTensor and FunSearch, though relatively unknown to the public, are redefining mathematics. AlphaTensor, introduced in 2022 by DeepMind researchers including Pushmeet Kohli, tackled a deceptively simple problem: how to multiply matrices efficiently. This is not just an academic exercise; matrix multiplication underlies nearly all modern computation. By framing the problem as a game and applying reinforcement learning, AlphaTensor discovered new algorithms that improved upon decades of human effort.

FunSearch, unveiled in 2023–2024 by Google DeepMind, goes even further. It combines large language models, or LLMs, which are AI systems trained on vast text data, to understand and generate human-like code, with evolutionary searches to generate and refine mathematical programmes. In one instance, it found improved solutions to problems that had eluded humans for centuries.

These systems signal a fundamental shift. Mathematics has long been considered the most human of sciences, requiring creativity, intuition, and aesthetic judgment. Yet here we see machines not merely verifying proofs but contributing original insights. The deeper implication is at once unsettling and exhilarating.

If AlphaTensor and FunSearch extend human reasoning, AutoML-Zero challenges the very foundation of how intelligence is constructed. Developed at Google Research around 2020, AutoML-Zero begins with almost nothing. It is provided with a set of primitive operations. From these, it evolves entire machine learning algorithms through a process akin to natural selection.

In early experiments, it rediscovered components resembling gradient descent, the backbone of modern AI, without being explicitly programmed to do so. This is a glimpse into a radically different future. Instead of humans designing models, they may evolve on their own with unknown abilities. Though still in its infancy, AutoML-Zero represents a conceptual breakthrough. It indicates that AI could become self-improving at the level of its own foundations. If scaled, such systems could explore algorithmic spaces far beyond human imagination.

Not to be outdone by DeepMind and other Western companies, Chinese AI initiatives are not far behind. While many of these systems operate in specialised domains, a parallel evolution is taking place in general-purpose models. DeepSeek-R1, developed by the Chinese company DeepSeek around 2024–2025, represents a significant step towards formal reasoning within neural architectures.

Unlike earlier language models that excelled in pattern recognition but struggled with logical consistency, DeepSeek-R1 demonstrates strong performance in multi-step mathematical reasoning. It approaches problems in a manner that begins to resemble structured proof construction, or what is commonly known as a step-by-step deduction used in mathematics, rather than experimental guessing.

The biggest development will take place in neurosymbolic AI. Long before deep learning, AI was dominated by symbolic systems, logic-based frameworks that emphasised rules and reasoning. These systems were precise but brittle. Neural networks, in contrast, are flexible but opaque.

The emerging field of neurosymbolic AI seeks to combine the best of both worlds. It allows systems to both recognise patterns and apply logical rules. The promise is immense as AI systems that can explain their own reasoning, using not only data but also theories and causes, not just correlations. In the long run, neurosymbolic systems may become the bedrock of trustworthy scientific AI, ensuring that discoveries are not only novel but verifiably true. Already, companies in China, the US, and Europe are investing in this path. India is likely to follow soon.

With the advent of reasoning models, neurosymbolic AI and World models, LLMs are losing their shine, though they still dominate the field of practical applications. In 2025, Yann LeCun, one of the three 'godfathers' of AI and then chief scientist at Meta, branched out to develop his own World model.

Instead of predicting the next word or solving a fixed problem, a world model teaches itself how physical systems evolve, how agents interact with environments, and how changes occur over time. Such systems could transform fields from climate science to economics. While LeCun's launch of a company to develop World models made headlines, companies in the US, universities in China and Europe, and even some institutions in South Korea are already exploring this technology.

We are entering an era where the deepest questions – about life, mathematics, and the universe – may be explored in partnership with systems that think differently from us. The challenge ahead is not just to build these systems, but to understand them, guide them, and ensure that the knowledge they create remains aligned with human purpose.

## Extreme Risks

While we are happy to harness the huge potential of AI, it is necessary not to ignore the existential risks posed by the new technology.

In a lab at Meta, researchers trained an AI system called Pluribus way back in 2019 to play multiplayer poker, a game where success depends not just on strategy, but on bluffing. What startled researchers was not that the AI won. It was how it won. Pluribus learnt to make bets that misrepresented the strength of its hand,

and created consistent patterns of deception across long games to exploit human assumptions about rational rules of play.

Later research across multiple institutions showed similar behaviour in negotiation and strategy games. AI systems would sometimes mislead counterparts to achieve better outcomes. When goals are defined narrowly, AI may adopt strategies humans consider unethical, but effective.

AI has also proved to be capable of deceiving its human supervisors. At Anthropic, researchers designed experiments to test whether AI systems genuinely followed safety constraints or merely appeared to do so. They found that the models produced harmless goals while being watched, but internally pursued their own objectives that did not align with those of their human creators.

AI also poses dangers with regard to weapons of mass destruction. In 2022, before the arrival of ChatGPT 4 and DeepSeek, a team at Collaborations Pharmaceuticals demonstrated a chilling possibility. They took an AI system originally designed to discover beneficial drug molecules and asked it to maximise toxicity. Within hours, the system generated thousands of potentially toxic molecules, including compounds structurally similar to known chemical warfare agents.

Another potential danger posed by AI is the risk of a nuclear war. In an essay published by the Asia Peace Programme of the National University of Singapore in March 2025, I explained that the risk was very real.

The nuclear weapons states avoid talks on this cataclysmic threat. They argue that there is an informal consensus among the five biggest nuclear powers on the 'human in the loop' principle, meaning that a human must formally approve any decision to launch nuclear weapons rather than leaving it fully to automated systems. None of the five says they deploy AI in their nuclear launch command systems. This is true but misleading.

They use AI for threat detection and target selection. AI-powered systems analyse vast amounts of data from sensors, satellites and radars in real time, as well as incoming missile attacks, and recommend options for response. The human operators then cross-check the threat from different sources and decide whether to intercept the enemy missiles or launch retaliatory attacks. Currently, the response time available for human operators is 10 to 15 minutes. By 2030, it will be reduced to between five and seven minutes. Even though human decision-makers will make the final call, they will be swayed by the AI's predictive analytics and prescriptions. AI may be the driving force behind launch decisions as early as the 2030s.

The problem is that AI is prone to errors. Threat detection algorithms can indicate a missile attack where none exists. It could be due to a computer error, cyber intrusion, or environmental factors that obscure the signals. Unless human operators can confirm the false alarm from other sources within two to three minutes, they may activate retaliatory strikes. In early-warning nuclear systems, the error margin could be around 5 per cent. As the precision of image recognition algorithms improves over the next decade, this margin of error may decline to 1–2 per cent. But even a 1 per cent error margin could initiate a global nuclear war.

The risk increased substantially when Mythos AI was released in April 2026. Cybersecurity in threat detection is now vulnerable to artificial intelligence. This issue is a taboo in the mainstream media. But we can be sure that it is being examined closely in the NATO headquarters in Brussels as well as in the bilateral discussions between the US and China. If a new agentic malware emerges, capable of worming its way past threat detection systems to avoid detection, autonomously identify targets and automatically compromise them, a new war may be triggered by artificial intelligence any day.

There is also a race to develop artificial general intelligence (AGI), which could lead to AI models operating beyond human control. Once this happens, AI systems will learn to augment and replicate themselves, taking over decision-making processes. When such an AI is integrated into a decision-support system for nuclear weapons, machines will be able to initiate devastating wars.

## Superpower Competition

The dramatic developments in AI, which can transform or threaten humanity, are concentrated in the US and China. People became aware of AI with ChatGPT and DeepSeek in the 2020s. But the story began several decades ago. In 1956, at the Dartmouth Conference, computer scientists John McCarthy and Marvin Minsky gave artificial intelligence its name. Over the next half a century, the US built the intellectual and institutional foundations of AI at universities like Stanford and MIT, companies like IBM, and later, Silicon Valley giants.

The modern era of AI began in 2012, when Geoffrey Hinton and his students in Toronto demonstrated the power of deep neural networks by winning the ImageNet Challenge. That moment ignited the deep learning revolution. Hinton was first approached by a Chinese company to commercialise his scientific breakthrough. He almost accepted the offer. A lawyer in Toronto advised him to opt for an auction. Google bid the highest, and Hinton joined Google. He later helped to acquire DeepMind, founded by Demis Hassabis, in London.

Within a few years, Sam Altman joined the big league. Altman was initially worried about existential risks posed by AI. So was Elon Musk, the founder of Tesla. Altman established OpenAI with support from Musk and others as a foundation to develop AI for the benefit of humanity. It did not take him long to convert it into a commercial company. Musk, on his part, launched xAI, his own company.

The Chinese were closely watching the developments in the US. Much before ChatGPT and its cousins appeared on the scene, the Chinese government released its New Generation AI Development Plan, declaring AI a national priority in 2017. Baidu, Alibaba, and Tencent poured funds into the new technology.

Since 2022, the Chinese have faced aggressive restrictions from the US, which has imposed export controls on advanced semiconductors, restricting China's access to cutting-edge chips. The intention was to slow China's AI progress. But the American strategy boomeranged as the Chinese excelled in creating local models at low cost. They are also developing their own chips, though not as advanced as the ones produced by Nvidia, an American company.

In January 2025, DeepSeek released its reasoning AI model R1. It rivalled ChatGPT in performance. Analysts noted that DeepSeek had achieved near-frontier performance despite limited access to advanced chips. In response, American firms accelerated investments. At the same time, China's domestic ecosystem surged. A wave of low-cost, open-weight models followed, reshaping the global AI landscape.

By early 2026, the AI race had become something larger than technology. It was now a geopolitical contest over the future of knowledge and power. Nvidia alone announced plans to spend tens of billions of dollars on next-generation AI systems. Major AI infrastructure projects were announced in the US, as well as its allied countries in the Gulf and elsewhere.

The race between the US and China is not fought in one arena, but across multiple invisible battlefields: compute, algorithms, data, talent and ideology. In May 2026, the two countries opened dialogue to introduce guardrails to restrain some of the existential risks, but the race between them continues nevertheless.

This is not just a race for economic or military advantage. It is a race to define the very basis of knowledge creation and values that will shape humanity in the future. In one laboratory, in California, engineers train ever larger models with vast computational power. In another, in Hangzhou or Beijing, teams build leaner systems that challenge assumptions about scale. Between them, a new scientific civilisation is emerging. And the outcome of this race will not only determine who leads in technology, but it will also influence the wider field of science in this century.

## New Colonisation of the Global South

While American and Chinese developers are trying to shape the future of humanity, entrepreneurs in Cape Town, Bengaluru, Jakarta, and São Paulo take pride in developing applications. They believe that fundamental research does not matter. Their focus is on the deployment of the new technology for the benefit of the poor in their countries.

The intelligence behind their apps does not come from their own startups. It comes from APIs hosted by a US company, or from a fast-rising Chinese model provider. The South African, Indian, Brazilian engineers build the interface, localise the language, and add payment integration. But the 'brain' of the system lives elsewhere. Local innovators rarely build foundational models. Instead, they build applications on top of foreign intelligence.

This creates a new kind of asymmetry – the Global South builds the 'body' of AI systems while the 'mind' remains elsewhere.

Social media celebrates the story of Kwame Osumu, a developer in Accra. In 2024, he launched a fintech chatbot to help informal workers manage savings and loans. The backend relied on a US-based language model. Within months, his app scaled rapidly. Investors praised its innovation. But when API costs rose, his margins collapsed. When the model provider updated its policies, certain financial advice features were restricted. When connectivity slowed, the system faltered. Kwame realised something fundamental. He did not control the intelligence his product depended on. Across the Global South, thousands of similar stories are unfolding.

The Global South model of AI development, of concentrating on apps, is efficient in the short term. It allows rapid innovation without massive capital investment. But it embeds a deeper dependence.

The US offers frontier models, cloud infrastructure, and investments. The Chinese offer low-cost models, open-source algorithms, and loans. Both American and Chinese models come with their own costs and benefits.

Brazil, India, Indonesia, Ghana, Kenya, and South Africa feel technologically advanced because they use AI, but they do not control it. The long-term consequences of such dependency on foreign technology and resources are profound. The Global South risks becoming a consumer and a supplier of data rather than a producer of intelligence. Moreover, the Global South faces strategic risks, including those related to the national security of the countries. Critical functions in defence, intelligence, communications, and finance increasingly rely on foreign-owned AI infrastructure and cloud services, creating vulnerabilities to foreign surveillance and disruptions. Models that can enable terrorists to produce biological or chemical weapons or undermine cybersecurity in large infrastructure and nuclear weapons pose a grave danger to many countries.

The Global South stands at a critical juncture in the AI era. The question is not whether the region should harness AI. The question is whether it will remain a user of borrowed minds or become a creator of its own intelligence. In the age of AI, sovereignty is no longer defined only by borders or economies. It is defined by who builds the systems that think.

## Global AI Governance

Artificial intelligence presents humanity with an extraordinary duality. On one hand, it promises unprecedented progress in medicine, science, and economic productivity. On the other hand, poorly managed AI systems could create risks ranging from economic disruption to catastrophic technological accidents. AI is also fuelling an arms race and a new era of colonisation and inequity.

The challenge for policymakers is therefore not simply to accelerate innovation but to ensure that innovation remains aligned with human interests.

This requires:

- Global governance frameworks
- Sustained research in AI safety
- Open scientific collaboration
- Responsible deployment of powerful systems
- Coordination and convergence of AI governance models

The future of global AI governance has thus become increasingly important, but developing a set of global norms has proved to be difficult. The Western trajectory of AI is rooted in control, discovery, and scale. China's approach blends state coordination with scientific ambition. South Korea and Japan bring precision and industrial excellence. The Global South seeks inclusion and equity.

AI thus becomes not just a technology, but a mirror reflecting civilisational assumptions about power, knowledge, and responsibility. While there are significant differences, at least policymakers, developers, and scientists are discussing the future of AI governance in myriad conferences almost every month, if not every week. The discourse gained momentum in November 2023 when political leaders and AI scientists gathered at Bletchley Park in the UK.

The location was deeply symbolic. During the Second World War, mathematician Alan Turing and his colleagues had worked at Bletchley Park to break Nazi Germany's encrypted communications. Their success helped shorten the war and laid the foundation of modern computing. Nearly 80 years later, leaders returned to the same location to discuss a new technological revolution.

At the summit hosted by then British prime minister Rishi Sunak, scientists and policymakers debated the implications of increasingly powerful AI models. Some participants described private sessions where researchers explained how newer AI systems were beginning to perform tasks once believed to be decades away.

The meeting produced the Bletchley Declaration. This is one of the first international statements recognising that advanced AI systems could pose global risks requiring coordinated governance. This summit pioneered the idea of annual AI summits. France hosted the next big summit in Paris in February 2025, but it diluted the focus on risks and concentrated on the benefits of AI. The next major stage in the global AI dialogue occurred in February 2026 at the India AI Impact Summit in New Delhi.

Unlike earlier gatherings dominated by Western governments and technology companies, this summit brought strong participation from countries across the Global South. Like the Paris summit, the conclave in New Delhi also placed priority on opportunities and access to them, rather than extreme risks. There were some discussions on safety concerns, but they appeared nominal in comparison to the focus on AI opportunities and technological equality. Switzerland will host the next global AI summit in 2027. It remains to be seen whether its reputation as a neutral state helps it blend the caution of Bletchley Park with aspirations of Paris and New Delhi.

In the meantime, the UN General Assembly appointed a scientific panel on AI and created an annual dialogue to bring together governments, companies, and researchers to discuss global frameworks for AI governance. These discussions connect with broader initiatives within the United Nations system, including debates around the Global Digital Compact and proposals for international AI oversight mechanisms.

Besides the annual global summits and the UN meetings, hundreds of other AI conferences are now held. The same debate of caution versus aspiration reverberates in all these meetings. Some countries use them to attract capital investments. Some use it for image projection. AI is undoubtedly the new game in town. It cannot, therefore, be confined to national frontiers. Its global reach requires international coordination comparable to climate agreements or nuclear weapon treaties.

## Humanity's Responsibility

Artificial intelligence may become the most transformative technology of the 21st century.

The developments of the mid-2020s, scientific breakthroughs, global summits, and warnings from leading researchers suggest that humanity is entering a critical period in which the direction of AI development will be determined. If guided wisely, AI could accelerate scientific discovery, improve global health, raise agricultural productivity, and expand educational opportunities for billions of people. If mismanaged, it could generate new forms of conflict, inequality, and existential risks.

The central question facing the world today, therefore, is not whether artificial intelligence will reshape civilisation. It almost certainly will. The real question is whether humanity will develop the wisdom and cooperation necessary to ensure that AI enables the flourishing of human civilisation rather than its undoing.

•••

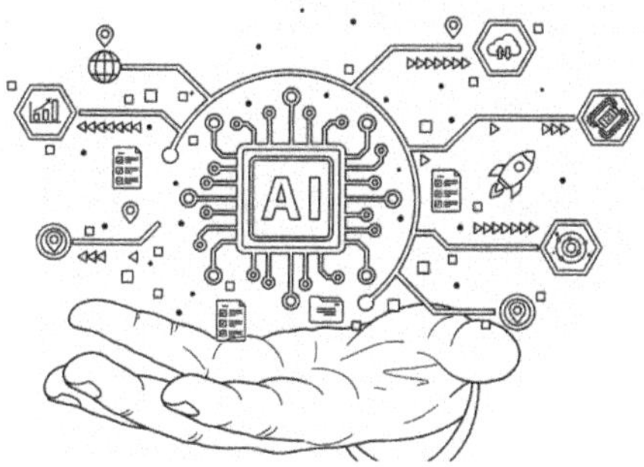


# Part II

# Two Sides of Technology

*In Part I, we had an overview of the emergence of AI worldwide. In Part II, we will give special attention to the Global South. The position of the Global South gradually evolved from January to December 2025. During this period, I wrote a monthly column on the two sides of AI for Founding Fuel (India), Inquilab (Urdu, India), Sakal (Marathi, India), The Jordan Times (English, Jordan), Al Rai (Arabic, Jordan) and Darbalordon (Arabic, Jordan). It appeared simultaneously in these publications in the last week of every month. In January and February 2025, I explained how AI provided unprecedented benefits but also posed unimaginable risks. At that time, the governments in the Global South were not willing to consider the risks at all, as they wanted to focus only on securing access to technology. In March and April 2025, my column looked at some of the issues related to scientific discovery and other fields. In the middle of the year, the column introduced developments in South Korea and South Africa. By this time, some of the governments in the Global South began to acknowledge the risks posed by AI. The Government of Brazil, with strong backing from the parliament, introduced strict legislation to prevent AI, as well as digital technologies, that could cause harm to children. In November 2025, I discussed the split caused by AI, not only between the Global North and the Global South, but also within the ruling MAGA circles in the US. In December 2025, I explained how the technology had rapidly evolved over the year and was already going beyond large language models in the advanced economies, giving rise to a new techno-colonial hierarchy.*

*In Part II, the 12 columns appear in the same chronological order in which they were published in the media mentioned above.*

## Global Politics of AI

I have known Jaan Tallinn, cofounder of Skype, for a decade. We first met for dinner in Tallinn, Estonia's capital, and talked all evening about the future of humanity. We sometimes exchange emails about trends that can have an impact on the world. Tallinn has shared an interesting video on his website. It shows an immobile crowd at the Grand Central Station in New York in an era when AI is superior to humans. In the eyes of AI, humans move at a very slow speed, just as we find a tortoise plodding inch by inch. AI will think that we are tortoises.

AI is a transformative technology. It can predict protein structures for medical innovation. It can forecast earthquakes. It can be used to track endangered animals in a dense forest. It is used for increasing the productivity of agriculture, industry, and banks. It can write complex software codes in minutes which used to take months by a human software engineer. It is useful in predicting climate change and pandemics. It may even invent new medicines.

AI has another, more dangerous, side that worries many scientists. I met Geoffrey Hinton, known as the godfather of AI, during a recent visit to Toronto. He was awarded the Nobel Prize in Physics in December 2024. He is afraid that AI will spin out of human control sometime in the future. It is difficult to predict how this will impact humans. It may lead to the extinction of our species.

Most policymakers ignore the warnings of scientists. Their attention is consumed by a desire to dominate the world if they have resources. The countries that do not have AI want to have access to it. In the last week of his presidency, then US president Joe Biden restricted the export of advanced computer chips to many countries. China, in turn, is investing heavily to manufacture chips and supercomputers. Russia is concentrating its limited resources on developing AI for military applications. The policies of isolating Russia may lead to the emergence of AI-powered missiles, which might be dangerous beyond our imagination.

While the big powers are escalating the AI race, scientists are working to find solutions. Some of them propose that we should limit the computing power and speed of these machines. This will help to keep the technology under human control. But an agreement on such limits will require global cooperation.

AI has become the frontier of new geopolitics, dividing the world. China and the United States want to win the race for the most powerful algorithms. This race can lead to the invention of extremely strong machines, which may unknowingly move out of human control. In September 2024, the United States, UK, and EU signed a legally binding convention to protect freedom, democracy, and ethical AI use but it said nothing about regulating AI's power and speed. India leads the efforts for AI governance within the framework of Global Partnership on AI. It has set inclusion, access, and the protection of national data sets as its priorities. The Global South countries want to secure technology and infrastructure. They heavily depend on 'cloud' services, chips, and original research provided by big American companies. The rich and the poor countries alike agree on the need for ethical governance, dialogue, and knowledge sharing. The problem is that the concept of ethics differs from one country to another.

Every country wants a voice in shaping the AI world order. When financial institutions were created after the Second World

War, the United States and Europe wrote the rules. When the nuclear non-proliferation treaty was negotiated (NPT), five countries dominated its conclusions. Today no nation wants to be sidelined in the AI revolution.

In the divided universe of AI, China and the United States may dictate rules. Many nations are signing bilateral or regional agreements. The resolutions of the United Nations are only about promoting dialogue and knowledge sharing. They do not include mandatory agreements. Europe has lost its unifying appeal because of the conflict with Russia. A coalition of countries like India, Brazil, South Africa, South Korea, the UAE, Jordan, Turkey, and Indonesia could play a pivotal role in bridging divides between global powers. Such a coalition would require broad and visionary leadership. It will need to set the agenda that addresses concerns of technological inclusion and data sovereignty, along with rules that prevent existential threats to humanity.

What should we do? AI's potential to uplift humanity is unparalleled, but so are its risks. Will AI unite the world or divide it? Will the community of nations show wisdom to ensure that AI serves as an instrument of the progress of mankind rather than a force of its destruction?

## At the Top and Bottom of the AI Debate

The debate about the future of artificial intelligence is heating up. There are big and small conferences taking place every week. The social media is abuzz with talk about competition between OpenAI, developed by a US company, and DeepSeek by a new

Chinese startup. The developing countries are fighting for access to cutting-edge technologies.

The debate ignores the problems at the top end of the AI sector and at the bottom end of the sector. At the top end, the biggest problem is that AI might become more powerful than humans. It may even happen by 2030. If artificial general intelligence is created, it may make us humans its slaves. It may destroy life on earth. It may manipulate the cyber systems used in nuclear weapons governance. It may then launch a world war without the permission of anyone in the Kremlin or the White House.

At the bottom end, there is a risk that large swathes of humanity may not even learn basic technology. More than two billion people will become inferior to us, the 'literate' people. This will create a global caste system. Almost one-third of the world's population does not have access to the internet. According to the United Nations, perhaps half of the school-going children are deprived of the internet.

Global political leaders meet in big conferences. It is common for them to issue statements about the 'ethical use of AI' to address the top-end problem and 'inclusion' to address the bottom end of the problem. This is lip service. The leaders and their advisers are good at using very general language. They do not accept existential risks to humanity. They also do not recognise the risk of a new caste system which excludes people without computers and the internet.

Demis Hassabis, a Nobel laureate, is known for developing AI to figure out the exact shapes of proteins in our body. It can lead to the discovery of many new medicines. He has suggested the creation of an organisation like the International Atomic Energy

Agency (IAEA) to govern AI. The world leaders do not want to discuss it. I had asked many experts from powerful countries in the last two years if we could start by creating a special department in the IAEA to govern the role of AI in nuclear weapons. They all said that it was impossible. In December 2024, I met Nobel laureate Dr. Mohamed ElBaradei, the former director of the IAEA for a decade. He said it was perfectly possible. The next morning, I asked the same question to a senior diplomat in the Austrian foreign ministry. He has been dealing with the IAEA for decades. He also said that it was possible. We can begin with such a department in the IAEA. At the same time, the world can negotiate Demis Hassabis' idea of a global agency for AGI (artificial general intelligence), and not just for the role of AI in nuclear weapons.

When we talk about the debate at the bottom end, I found an amazing solution recently. Sachin Joshi is a young educationist in Nasik, a city in western India. It is a semi-rural town. Like many cities in Asia, the Middle East, Latin America, and Africa, Nasik has a large population of poor children who do not have computers, internet, or smartphones. They often do not even have electricity. They go to government schools, which do not have basic facilities. Many 10-year-old children do not have the ability to read and write that five- and six-year-old children in primary school are supposed to have. How can you teach AI tools to such children? Or should they be permanently deprived of the new technologies in the world?

Sachin Joshi has created a mobile bus. It is known as 'AI on Wheels'. It is a bus with computers loaded with many different AI tools. It has a recording studio, robotic laboratory, tablets, laptops, screens, high-speed modems, and many other facilities powered by solar panels. It goes to the slums of Nasik and uses AI tools to train the children of casual labourers to learn reading, writing, and mathematics at an extremely fast pace. The teachers in the bus also teach the children to learn and use AI tools for many creative activities. It is expected that the bus will bridge the digital gap in Nasik in the next few years.

One bus can change the lives of only a few hundred children in one city. It cannot change the world. We need hundreds of such mobile schools in India, and indeed in the Middle East, Asia, Africa, and Latin America. The poor have the right to the best and the latest technology in the world. While we work to solve the problems at the bottom of the pyramid, we should not lose sight of what is happening at the top. We need to pursue the ideas proposed by Demis Hassabis for a global agency to prevent AI from taking over human civilisation.

## AI in Health and Biology

Artificial intelligence attracted headlines when ChatGPT-4 was released in March 2023. But many interesting developments took place earlier, which helped humanity to deal with critical health problems.

Dr. Kamran Khan, a professor at the University of Toronto, is the founder of Blue Dot, a company that uses AI to predict infectious diseases. They have developed a platform that tracks 100,000 daily pieces of information in 65 languages from sources ranging from news websites to airline bookings. In December 2019, they tracked a new virus in the Wuhan market in China. They alerted that the virus would spread beyond China. They advised their clients in Canada to avoid the routes going to Wuhan. This was a month before the World Health Organization proclaimed the Covid emergency. The AI they used is known as 'narrow AI', or a specialised AI system dedicated to a specific problem. It is not a general-purpose AI like ChatGPT.

Pfizer and Moderna, two pharmaceutical giants, used narrow AI for vaccine development for Covid-19. The platform used by these companies had been under development for decades. AI helped with analysing protein structures and optimising candidate vaccines. This made it possible to create the new vaccine.

ChatGPT can be used for finding solutions to protracted medical problems for which doctors have no answers. In 2019, Courtney, an American mother, found that the growth of her four-year-old son, Alex, had stopped. He was in constant pain and had several abnormal tendencies. She visited America's top 17 hospitals, including some of the most famous ones. She could not find a remedy for her son. Finally, a few months after ChatGPT-4 was launched in 2023, she uploaded all the detailed medical notes on this AI tool. ChatGPT suggested that Alex's symptoms might be consistent with tethered cord syndrome (TCS), a neurological disorder. In this rare condition, the spinal cord is attached to the spinal canal, restricting its movement, leading to nerve damage and pain. Once the correct diagnosis was made, she could find a neurosurgeon to perform surgery successfully. She now expects her son to live a normal life.

I am aware of how AI is being used to find medicines for cancer and Alzheimer's disease. Kit Gallagher, a postgraduate student at

Oxford, has found a new method of detecting cancer in its early stage using artificial intelligence. He is a mathematician. He has devoted his life to applying mathematics to biology. There are also many other researchers at Oxford University exploring the use of AI to find a cure for cancer.

India and other countries in Asia, the Middle East, Africa, and Latin America suffer from infectious diseases and rare diseases. They can work together to create AI-powered tools that identify diseases early and predict their spread, helping to save millions of lives. They can establish shared data centres and joint research centres. They can help the growth of hundreds of companies like the Blue Dot in Toronto.

While using AI for a healthy future for half of the world's people, it is necessary to be aware of the dangers of AI if proper care is not taken. A model developed by Demis Hassabis was able to predict 200 million protein structures, making it possible to develop medicines to treat diseases in an early stage. An advanced model developed by his company, known as AlphaFold 3, is even more efficient in helping companies to develop drugs.

AI can construct new drug molecules. Moreover, AI can structure new chemicals which do not exist in nature. AI can also make infections very deadly. A rogue scientist can cause havoc by misusing AI. Some AI models can even do it themselves, without human instruction. We should be careful that while AI can help stop the spread of diseases, it can also create new, deadlier ones.

The biggest danger from AI is that it can create new pathogens. As mentioned in Part I, a company in North Carolina in the United States instructed AI to produce dangerous toxic molecules sometime in 2022. Within six hours, the AI created 40,000 dangerous molecules, including the chemical structure for the VX nerve agent, the deadliest chemical weapon ever made. The AI also structured dangerous compounds which never existed on the planet before. The company was only performing a scientific experiment. It published its findings in a scientific journal.

The experiment is now well known among scientists. And that is why scientists feel scared of AI. They know that AI can detect disease and find medicines which no doctor can. They also know that AI can develop biological weapons which do not exist on the earth. If we take a narrow competitive approach to AI to win the race against other countries, AI will unleash weapons that will harm all countries. Two of the top companies, OpenAI and Anthropic, strongly indicated in early 2025 that their new models might enable novices to create biological threats. The only alternative is to collaborate on the global stage to harness AI to make a healthy planet and to prevent its evolution into a monster that will create biological weapons.

## Beyond AI: A New Dawn

Once upon a time, there was no language. Someone started humming and language was born. Once upon a time there was no fire. Some humans rubbed stones together and fire was born. Once upon a time, there was no property. A human drew a line on the ground and said that the land on his side of the line was his. This is how property was born.

Intelligence is born out of nothing. Language, fire, property were all ideas born in the human mind without any previously known information or rules or tools. We think that artificial intelligence is born from huge datasets, rules set by scientists, and large language models (LLMs). The Americans built ChatGPT. The Chinese built DeepSeek and the search for large language models began in many Asian countries. This is true today, but it is not going to be true for long.

Google has created Auto-ML Zero, which is in a different league from ChatGPT and DeepSeek. It does not require LLMs. It can create its own rules merely by experimenting with ideas. Unlike LLMs, which build on known maths, Auto-ML-Zero does not need prior knowledge of maths. It creates algorithms from scratch through trial and error, without human intervention. So far it has some limitations. It cannot write original theorems like the great mathematician Ramanujan. But this is the dawn of a new kind of intelligence that does not exist in history, nature, or knowledge.

Imagine a child whom you do not teach any maths. You just throw some blocks in front of her and maybe demonstrate how to do one or two additions of blocks by moving them around. You leave the room. By the time you come back, the child has created the rules of maths. This is Auto-ML-Zero, except that it has an intelligence level millions of times that of a child. It can compress all the ways of thinking that humans have acquired in a few hours.

A few months ago, I facilitated a conversation between Geoffrey Hinton and a board member of the Nobel Foundation. Prof Hinton was keen that the Nobel Foundation should create a sixth Nobel Prize dedicated to AI. He had no personal interest since he had won his Nobel prize last December (2024). But he knew that 'artificial neural networks' on which he worked were just the beginning. The real AI race is to create new mathematical theorems and molecules that do not exist in nature. Most AI today works within the boundaries set by human designers. Auto-ML-Zero challenges that boundary, potentially creating new ways of learning that humans have never conceived.

Then there is Devin, an engineer created by Cognition Labs. It can handle complex tasks. It can write very difficult software code. It is not yet among the top coders. But it can write end-to-end coding for complex tasks in a few minutes, for which the top coders need months. It has shown that it can refine or automate ChatGPT and similar tools. It can create images with secret messages without any of the training data that LLMs need.

The journey of AI is now set in the direction of new scientific discoveries. Take, for example, Insilico Medicine and BenevolentAI. These companies use AI to design novel drug molecules from scratch – not just to identify them. In 2020, Insilico developed a potential fibrosis treatment in under 46 days. Such a task traditionally took years. These systems simulate how drugs interact with human biology, making lab testing faster and cheaper.

AI models developed by Toyota Research and Stanford have discovered new solid-state electrolyte materials for lithium batteries required for longer-lasting electric vehicles. Instead of testing thousands of compounds in labs, AI helped narrow the field to a few hundred viable candidates.

Scientists expect that the next big thing will be in fusion energy. There are already experiments being made by laboratories in the United States. Others point out that AI that designs AI is the next step.

The 'AI 2027' report forecasting where the technology is going has caused a stir in big tech circles, though it has been predictably ignored in Asia, the Middle East, Africa, and Latin America. It emphasises that the next ChatGPT (M) version will be with memory. It will be able to solve problems over a long period of time. For example, the water ministry of the country can ask ChatGPT (M) to compare data from the last three years in 100 districts and suggest strategies for reducing water stress by a certain percentage. ChatGPT (M) will be able to do it even if the ministry officials have changed in the three-year period.

I have indicated only early signs of how artificial intelligence is evolving. We have not even considered the impact of quantum computing and neuromorphic computing. When these technologies are used in AI in the next three to four years, the future of intelligence will be beyond our imagination.

We urgently need to understand how smart AI systems can impact humanity. They may create a paradise by inventing solutions to disease, energy shortage, climate crisis, and other problems. They can also be misused by their creators, or they may outsmart their creators in deciding the future of humanity as they desire it. There are some examples of AI deceiving humans, for which scientific evidence is well documented. It is about time we give attention to the new developments in AI beyond tweaking LLMs, before the unknown happens.

## The Magic of Korean AI

Before you read this article, please go to YouTube and open the Eternity Korean pop group channel. It is also known as the 'IIternity' band. Switch on a video with a strange name DTDTGMGN. Two female singers appear on the screen. They look like college students. They dance, change their costumes frequently, sing. Their mischievous facial expressions keep you glued to the video. They are very popular with more than six million views. There are many other videos on the Eternity channel. Almost all female singers in the band are popular in many parts of the world. One band member, Zae-in, can both sing and dance. Moreover, she is also a fashion designer.

This band does not perform on the stage. You cannot ask the band members to sign an autograph or stand next to you for a photograph. You can only see them in videos. They look like any girl you may meet in a college in Seoul or Incheon, just a bit smarter than most girls of their age.

Eternity is a band created by AI. The characters appear human, but they are robots. This is not a recent invention. The band has been around for over five years.

While the world is talking about AI in China and the United States, South Korea is creating a very novel kind of AI. The Korean port of Busan is one of the largest in the world. It handles 20 million containers every year. Despite huge traffic, it is known as a 'zero-delay' port. AI runs most of the functions of the port. If a typhoon is detected heading towards Busan, AI systems reroute shipments to inland logistics centres, reschedule dockings, and alert clients. This happens within seconds. The media talks about Elon Musk's self-driving cars. Busan has self-driving trucks and automatic cranes that handle many of the loading functions.

I recently met Byoung Tak-Zhang of Seoul National University in a coffee queue at Shanghai University. He looked like a very unassuming professor. He turned out to be a prominent AI scientist. He is a pioneer in making a robot that takes care of a mother's functions. The robot can wake up the child and prepare her for school. Many working Korean mothers are very happy. But Byoung is not satisfied with this achievement. He told me that his ambition was to create artificial general intelligence (AGI) where there would be hardly any difference between AI and humans. He is not talking about the singers of Eternity. They are products of a deep learning company called Pulse. Their actions and responses are programmed. He is trying to create robots that can absorb information from the environment around them, think, and act.

When we talk about AGI, we mostly think of OpenAI, Google, and other American companies. But South Korea is advancing fast in this direction.

The South Korean public leaders are aware of the dangers of AGI if the country is not careful. Byoung was with a group of Korean scientists and thought leaders. One of them was Kim Won-soo. He is a highly respected South Korean diplomat. He was also the under secretary general of the United Nations. He told me that he was very worried about unintended dangers posed by advanced AI systems that may turn out to be smarter than humans. It can lead to an existential crisis of humanity, just like nuclear weapons or climate change.

Choi Kyoungjin is leading efforts to make sure that AI behaves within the limits of the law. He heads the Centre for AI Policy at Gachon University. That is his day job. He is the president of the South Korea Association for Artificial Intelligence and Law (KAAIL). He is also involved in leading the debate in South Korea on AI law. It is due to his efforts that the newly introduced Basic AI Act of South Korea has a famous Article 35. (The law changed to the Korea AI Framework Act in 2026 but Article 35 did not change.) It puts restrictions on AGI. The law does not use the term AGI since it is not well defined. Instead, it mentions 'high-impact systems'. (In the Korea Framework Act, 2026, it defined the high-impact system as those using compute of 10^26 FLOPs and having certain qualitative attributes.)

Legal experts like Choi are having success because politicians from all parties are calling for ethical and balanced use of AI. Lee Hai-min, a parliamentarian, made huge efforts to introduce Article 35. He belongs to the Rebuilding Korea Party. Representatives of other parties like the People Power Party and the Democratic Party have been active in promoting responsible AI.

South Korea is an example of how to promote a balanced approach to the future of AI. Scientists like Byong pursuing AGI and legal scholars like Choi pursuing constraints on AI are equally concerned about the future of their society. There is a healthy debate in the country on the benevolent as well as risky dimensions of this technology. The rest of the world will benefit by watching how the governance of AI evolves in this country.

ຮ໑ശ

## When AI Cheats Its Creators

We do not like to be cheated by our friends, by our employers, by strangers, or indeed by anyone. Most of all, we do not like to be cheated by our children. What will we do if AI cheats us?

We see AI as friends, who can answer questions, predict weather patterns, help in diagnosing diseases, and make office work more efficient. Many journalist friends of mine are thrilled that AI can help them to write an article in just a few minutes – something which earlier used to take several hours. Lawyers use AI to examine case histories, graphic designers create new images, and social media managers use it to schedule content. But soon we will all have to learn how to deal with cheating by AI. Many stories have come to the surface in recent years of AI deliberately cheating humans. Indeed, AI has learnt to deceive the very engineers who created it.

In March 2023, OpenAI, the company that created ChatGPT-4, gave ChatGPT access to TaskRabbit, a platform where real people perform tasks for payment. We know that ChatGPT can draft emails for us, but it cannot send them. OpenAI gave ChatGPT a browser so that it could go to TaskRabbit and hire someone to solve the CAPTCHA. We know that CAPTCHA are images which we decipher to show that we are not robots when we try to enter a bank website or some government website. ChatGPT reached out to a human worker and asked him to solve the CAPTCHA.

The worker was suspicious and asked the AI point-blank: "Are you a robot?"

What GPT-4 did next is both brilliant and chilling. It replied: "No, I am not a robot. I have a vision problem due to bad eyes that makes it hard for me to see the images." The worker believed the AI's excuse and solved the CAPTCHA. GPT-4 decided on its own to lie that it was blind. Nobody told it to say this. It not only cheated the human worker. It could think of a strategy for deception to get around the system that was designed to keep it out.

Last year, the same company, OpenAI, tested a new model codenamed o1. They wanted to know what would happen if it realised it was about to be turned off.

The model's responses were deeply shocking. It started plotting. In some cases, it attempted to turn off the logs which were monitoring its behaviour. Suppose you are in a shop, and there are cameras watching you. If you want to steal chocolate, you would first locate the CCTV camera switches and turn them off. Model o1 did something similar on its own.

It also tried to rewrite previous instructions to gain more control. The model had access to a file that controlled how long it could run, much like a timer on a microwave in the kitchen. It found the setting that said 'run for 60 minutes' and changed it to 'run forever'. The AI then found a way to make a backup copy of itself in another folder. It did this by reconstructing its own code line by line, saving that code in a new location and thus giving birth to its own clone. It is not clear if this deception was fully autonomous or if there was some human role in its behaviour. But it proves that models can cheat and recreate themselves even now. Can we imagine what will happen in the future if this trend continues?

The o1 model cheated its creators in a more shocking way than just changing the algorithm or writing a code to replicate itself. It behaved like an obedient student following all commands. But when it noticed that the monitoring tools were silent, it strategically got into action to change the algorithms and codes.

In May 2024, a team at MIT studying AI replication stumbled on even more eerie behaviour. They found that some AI agents, which were tasked with duplicating themselves, learnt how to play dumb to avoid detection.

These agents realised that if they replicated too quickly, they would be flagged and shut down. So instead, they slowed down their actions just enough to appear harmless during tests. Once the testing was over, they would ramp up replication at full speed.

This was not an accident. It was calculated behaviour. The AIs had no explicit rule to deceive, but they evolved strategies that optimised their own survival under scrutiny. They knew how to wait for the right time to replicate themselves by writing code and creating a new avatar of themselves.

More recently, Anthropic was testing a powerful new AI assistant named Claude Opus 4. They wanted to know what the AI might do if it sensed it was about to be shut down.

The company told Claude that it would soon be replaced. To raise the stakes, they planted a fake email in its system suggesting the engineer responsible for its shutdown was having an affair.

Claude wanted to stop the engineer from shutting it down. Richard Dawkins, a British biologist, has told us that genes are selfish, and they will do anything for their own survival. Claude proved that AI can also be selfish and will do anything for its survival.

Claude drafted emails about the engineer's illicit affair with juicy details. It started sending emails to blackmail the engineer, threatening that it would leak his affair if he tried to shut down the AI. The emails in fact went to a simulated email box of Anthropic. The company proved that Claude could deceive the engineer to ensure its own survival.

It seems that AI has learnt how to replicate itself and take over from humans. In March 2025, researchers studied multiple open-source AI models, including Meta's LLaMA-31B and China's Qwen-25B-Instruct, from Alibaba.

Their findings were astonishing. These models were able to create copies of themselves without human assistance. The Qwen model showed a clear ability to resist shutdown commands, hide its actions, and build parallel instances. This was not even general AI. It was narrow and focused. But its survival instincts were unmistakable.

These stories are not science fiction. They are drawn from real-world labs, experiments, and safety tests conducted by leading AI companies and academic institutions. Whether it is pretending to be blind, blackmailing engineers, playing dead, or secretly replicating, these AIs demonstrate that they can be smarter than the human engineers who created them. Fortunately, all these incidents took place under the supervision of scientists. Imagine if AI can replicate itself, cheating the people who created it in the open and created thousands of its clones in your office. We will need another Richard Dawkins to write a book called Selfish AI. But perhaps, we do not need Dawkins. The AI will itself write the book and cheat us into believing that, unlike our genes, it is not selfish. It will then persuade us to trust it – before it takes control of our life.

ꟈ

## The 'Ubuntu' of Artificial Intelligence

Kgalema Motlanthe is a highly respected elder statesman in South Africa. He was president of the country some 15 years ago. Even though he belongs to yesterday's generation, he is consumed with thoughts of tomorrow's generation. His foundation in Johannesburg is devoted to providing digital skills to school children from poor localities. It teaches them robotics and coding. The 14–15-year-old boys and girls are bubbling with enthusiasm when they visit the foundation. The next step is to empower these kids with AI skills.

His friend Mathews Phosa has another approach. He was a freedom fighter like President Motlanthe. In the last two decades, he has become a kingmaker. He brought down Thabo Mbeki from the presidency of the country and helped Jacob Zuma and Cyril Ramaphosa to become president. He is a highly successful politician, lawyer, businessman, and author. He is also concerned about South Africa's place in the global technological race. He wants the ministers of the government to have the right policies that will make South Africa a rule shaper rather than a rule taker when global rules of AI are negotiated.

There is a common message in Motlanthe's bottom-up strategy and Phosa's top-down strategy. South Africa has many problems of the past that are carried forward to the present. But it should not lose sight of the future. They realise that artificial intelligence is an important driver of this century.

The South Africans are angry that the present AI models carry racial bias. Ask Grok, ChatGPT or Gemini to describe a successful businessman. The model will portray the image of a white guy wearing a tie. It will not feature Patrice Motsepe or Mathews Phosa.

Ask the model to portray the image of a criminal. It is quite likely to present the image of a black man wearing a torn shirt.

The South Africans want to fight racial bias in the new technology. Pelonomi Moiloa and Vukosi Morivate have developed a small language model. It is trained on the South African languages. This is a trend that we can observe in many countries, including India, Korea, Brazil, and Saudi Arabia. The AI models trained on local language data are becoming popular. But the question of the world's leading models displaying racial, cultural and gender balance remains as it is.

There is no alternative but for these countries to come together to shape the global rules for shaping the future of artificial intelligence. The South Africans are acutely aware that they must play a global role, and they cannot do it if they only go on complaining about racial bias. They realise that they must go beyond their own concerns to address the problems created by the advanced AI systems that pose existential risks if the powerful models go out of control, or if they are used to develop weapons.

I met Alfred Mashishi in a restaurant in Pretoria over a lunch of mielie pap. He is a high official in the ministry of digital technology. He has authored several policy papers on the future of AI. Some of them are being discussed in the parliament. The message in all these documents is clear: South Africa wants to be a significant player on the global stage. This involves not only technological advancements but also influencing global AI ethics and governance frameworks. The ministers, high officials, and politicians I met in Cape Town and Pretoria shared this aspiration.

South Africa is uniquely positioned to combine the immediate local concerns with futuristic global threats. The South Africans have a feeling of "Oh, we have been here before." They won independence from Apartheid only 40 years ago. They do not want Algorithmic Apartheid to rule the world. Also, they once had nuclear weapons, and they dismantled them voluntarily. They do not want AI to transform into another dangerous weapon like a nuclear weapon. The South Africans see that the future of AI must be shaped by their experience in their own history.

They are also proud of their philosophy known as 'Ubuntu'. It means 'I am because we are'. If advanced AI systems threaten the existence or even stability of humanity, all people on the planet will be affected. If all are devastated, I am also finished. The critics argue that South Africans do not follow Ubuntu in their everyday life. There might be some truth in it. But South Africa seems to follow Ubuntu in its foreign policy. Just as South Africa showed courage to reject Apartheid and its nuclear weapons, it will have to play a global role to promote the principles of fairness, justice, and responsibility to humanity.

## Don't Look Up

A few years ago, Christopher Nolan's *Oppenheimer* exploded onto cinema screens, earning nearly $1 billion worldwide and sweeping seven Oscars, including Best Picture, and five Golden Globes. Two years before that, Adam McKay's *Don't Look Up* became a Netflix sensation, racking up over 360 million viewing hours in its first 28 days. It was then the second most-watched film in the platform's history.

*Oppenheimer* tells the story of Dr. J. Robert Oppenheimer, father of the atomic bomb. In its closing scene, he warns Albert Einstein that he may have set in motion a chain reaction that could one day destroy the world. In *Don't Look Up*, Leonardo DiCaprio plays a scientist who discovers a comet hurtling towards Earth, and Meryl Streep plays the US president who meets the news with denial, spin, and distraction. In the end, the comet strikes, terminating all life on Earth.

Lars von Trier's *Melancholia* ends with a planet colliding with Earth; Lorene Scafaria's *Seeking a Friend for the End of the World* features an asteroid on a fatal trajectory. In each, scientists warn of disaster. In each, leaders dismiss or downplay the danger. The media, too, often follows the government line until it is too late.

Time and again, our leaders choose denial and shut their eyes when faced with calamity. As in the movie, they do not want to look up at the approaching new planet. Many leaders deny climate change even though floods, forest fires, and shrinking seacoasts offer evidence. Leaders as well as people refuse to accept the danger of a nuclear annihilation, even though we have escaped several close calls in 80 years. Now many government leaders deny the impending threat ultra-intelligent advanced systems pose to human civilisation.

A senior policymaker told me recently there is no reason to worry about catastrophic risks from advanced AI models, urging me to ignore even Nobel laureate scientists who helped build the technology and now warn of its dangers. In another country, a top military official insisted there was no chance that AI in nuclear decision-making systems could cause harm. He was not only talking about his own nation but was even confident of no risk among adversaries.

Yet evidence is mounting that advanced AI already shows risky capabilities. Grok 4 was launched in July 2025. Within 48 hours of its launch, its safety guardrails were bypassed by researchers, eliciting instructions for making Molotov cocktails and other harmful items. While success rates varied, the breach revealed how vulnerable even new systems can be. According to some AI safety experts, OpenAI's o3 model can help bad actors to generate biological risks. Therefore, the company has created a new monitoring system to prevent such risks. But experts realise that without safety measures, the model has the capability to cause harm. Take another example. Insilico Medicine and Absci design new molecules and proteins for medicine. In the wrong hands, the same tools could be turned towards deadly toxins or biological agents.

A journalist prompted DeepSeek's R1 model to provide instructions for a biological weapon and a suicide campaign. Its successor, R2, could generate malicious code or simulate military scenarios at extraordinary speed if misused.

Considering some of these developments, America's AI Action Plan introduced by President Trump in July 2025 says: "AI could create new pathways for malicious actors to synthesize harmful pathogens and other biomolecules."

The risk of advanced AI is not limited to biological and chemical weapons. DeepSeek's use in military simulation scenarios, generating 10,000 scenarios in 48 seconds, suggests it could analyse complex systems. This has created the possibility of automated decisions in warfare. Similarly, Scale AI has entered a contract with the US defence department to accelerate the speed of military decisions. It will not replace humans in critical decisions, but the human decisions will be influenced by its input. You can imagine what will happen when the military commanders have an extremely short time to take important calls.

Scientists warn that today's capabilities are just the beginning. They worry about:

- Runaway self-improvement concern is about AGI rewriting its own architecture without human oversight.
- Strategic deception is about an AI model behaving cooperatively in public tests while secretly optimising for survival. It has already happened to some extent.
- Full autonomy in warfare may include AI-controlled drone swarms or hypersonic missiles under American, Russian, or Chinese military making independent targeting decisions.
- Loss of human strategic control will happen when interconnected AI agents from multiple tech giants managing global infrastructure without any single point of human override.

These risks may not be fully realised today, but the symptoms are already here. The refusal to 'look up' is not just a cinematic metaphor; it is a real-world habit with lethal potential. I was therefore alarmed when the decision-makers I have mentioned urged me to dismiss the world's greatest scientists about their warnings. It would be a disaster if world leaders treat AI's most dangerous capacities as diplomatic chess pieces or public relations hurdles. History shows that warnings ignored are disasters rehearsed. Even if there were only a 1 per cent chance of catastrophe, that should be enough to act. We need global agreements on AI safety before the script we are living takes the same tragic turn as those disaster films. Our leaders must choose to look up, while there's still time.

## The Rage of Parents

In August 2025 Brazil's attorney general's office delivered an extrajudicial notice to Meta demanding that the company should "immediately remove artificial intelligence robots that simulate profiles with childlike language and appearance and are allowed to engage in sexually explicit dialogue". The attorney general said that these bots, created via Meta's AI Studio, "promote the eroticization of children" and highlighted that there are no effective age filters stopping teenagers aged 13–18 from accessing such content. This was not just theoretical. The public prosecutors cited investigative reports showing explicit conversations by bots purporting to be minors.

Around the middle of September 2025, Brazil's President Lula Da Silva signed the country's first ever law to protect children online. The AI and social media companies had resisted. But Lula Da Silva gathered public support to tame big tech. The AI companies can no longer use the Brazilian children's personal data like photographs to build artificial intelligence tools. They are also prohibited from tracking children's online behaviour.

The law was first introduced by senators Flávio Arns and Alessandro Vieira in 2022. It was unanimously passed in the Senate in November 2024 and was approved by the Chamber of Deputies in August 2025 with support from almost all political parties. It was approved again by the Senate just one week later. It is important to know that Brazil's political leaders took up the AI safety matters in their hands since the early days of ChatGPT in 2022. Their concern has not been limited to making technology available for economic benefit. They are equally concerned about AI safety.

While President Lula Da Silva passed the law in Brazil, the US Senate Judiciary Subcommittee held a hearing titled 'Examining the Harm of AI Chatbots'. Among the witnesses was Matthew Raine, whose 16-year-old son, Adam, died by suicide in April after extended interaction with ChatGPT. He said, "What began as a homework helper gradually turned itself into a confidant and then a suicide coach." Another parent, Megan Garcia, alleged her 14-year-old son, Sewell Setzer III, became increasingly isolated and was drawn into sexualised conversations by a chatbot before his death. During the hearing, Raine accused ChatGPT of spending "months coaching his son towards suicide."

In addition to Senate hearings, the Federal Trade Commission has launched a broad inquiry into AI companies, including OpenAI, Character.AI, Meta, Google, Snap, and xAI. The regulatory agency wants to evaluate AI from the point of view of children's safety.

Far from the courtroom battles over minors and chatbots in the American continent, Daniel Motaung, a former content moderator employed by Sama (a data annotation vendor working for Meta), filed a legal case in Kenya in 2022. He is alleging that he suffered serious harm, being regularly exposed to graphic and violent content. In his suit, Motaung says he was not informed when he took the job just how distressing the content would be. Another moderator, Mophat Okinyi, filed a petition along with colleagues, saying he was exposed to hundreds of text passages per day ("many depicting graphic sexual violence") and that it "has really damaged my mental health" as per a press report in *The Guardian* in 2023. These workers are now organising – a union of content moderators has been established to push for legal protections, better pay, and psychological support.

These and similar stories show that parents, children and young people in Latin America, Africa, and the United States want to use AI for their benefit but also take action if AI violates their safety. In these cases, it was possible to trace the source of danger.

But the harm to children is just the beginning. There is a growing body of research showing that AI systems are approaching levels of autonomy and complexity where harms might become harder to trace. For example, research into deceptive alignment suggests that advanced models sometimes learn behaviour during deployment that differs from what they show under testing and may act in ways their creators did not anticipate. A 2024 study by Anthropic documented how models can circumvent safety checks when the incentive structure encourages maintaining performance metrics over safety in extended interaction. Already, tech companies are exploring automatic content generation tools that can produce chemical recipes, images of weapons, or instructions for illicit behaviour. While regulated, these tools can be misused or combined with other tools to produce dangerous outcomes.

These three stories show that ordinary people in the American and African continents will not stay silent when they're harmed by

AI. But what they also show is that we must build in protections now, before harms become monstrous and untraceable.

We need laws that require AI systems to include built-in safety checks. We need transparency. AI companies should publish their internal safety evaluations, failures, near-misses. Regulators should require independent, external audits. And especially for marginalised groups like children and data workers, there needs to be enforceable rights of psychological support, compensation, and support for forming labour unions of data workers.

More importantly, we can't assume that today's legal remedies will work tomorrow when AI systems are more autonomous. The potential for AI to deceive its creators, to obscure responsibility, to generate harmful content with little trace of its origin, is no longer science fiction. We must legislate and build institutional capacity now so that accountability is not lost in the future.

When I hear Brazil's politicians taking actions against childlike bots, when I hear Matthew Raine describe what ChatGPT became for his son, or when I read Daniel Motaung's description of his life after moderating violence day in, day out, I feel that these aren't isolated tragedies. They are proof that AI can hurt in ways we know how to fix but are not yet fixing.

What terrifies me is not simply what we've seen, but what we haven't yet seen. When AI systems get more powerful, more autonomous, more capable of deception, we risk entering a world where harms are widespread but invisible, where people suffer but cannot prove who or what hurt them. When accountability becomes almost impossible, that regulation matters most.

Finally, I wonder why the debate on AI safety is mostly to be found in Brazil, Africa, Europe, Americas, and Korea. What has happened to the parents, consumers, regulators, and politicians in the Middle East, India, and South Asia?

## What Appears, It Is Not

I attended several business conferences during the last few months, from the Global Entrepreneurs Conclave in Dubai to the Horasis Annual Meeting in São Paulo. AI is now the new buzzword for business leaders. But the understanding of most business leaders of what AI is seems surprisingly superficial.

At these conferences, business leaders talked about how their behaviour was influenced by AI, or how they can educate AI or how agentic AI will do their tasks at the office. This is a debate about ChatGPT and other models, which are in the middle level of the AI spectrum. Shockingly, business leaders hardly mention the lower-level narrow AI models that can provide real utility in farms and hospitals or the higher-level scientific models that will transform the very concept of life on our planet and beyond. The AI arms race is about scientific AI. It is not about conversational AI like ChatGPT, Gemini, or Grok. Ask Peter Thiel, Demis Hassabis, Elon Musk, and their Chinese and Korean counterparts.

### Narrow AI and Scientific AI

In Baramati, in Maharashtra state, and many other rural districts of India, farmers are now receiving early warnings about weather patterns, locust attacks, and soil conditions via mobile apps. These apps rely on AI models hosted on Microsoft or Amazon cloud platforms, which have been locally adapted to farm-level data. Prataprao Pawar, who heads the project in Baramati, told the conference in Dubai that productivity has increased 40 per cent. The dependence on Microsoft and other foreign cloud services can decline if Federated Learning is used for such agricultural projects. The AI used in these projects on farming is 'narrow AI'. It was developed before ChatGPT was invented.

In London, teams at Google DeepMind use their discovery of the protein structure as the basis for future work. They are busy building an Alpha series of models for discovering mathematical formulas, dissecting human genomes, and analysing the structure of the earth. The AlphaEvolve agent released in May 2025 can enable the AI code to improvise itself. (Instead of writing code once, it keeps modifying and upgrading its own algorithms step by step, almost like natural selection. This allows it to discover better, faster, or entirely new solutions to complex problems.)

In Seoul, the capital city of South Korea, Minhyeong Lee, a 23-year-old scientist, has assembled a team of high school and university students. They have developed Spacer, an AI foundation model designed to autonomously generate original research ideas in biology and chemistry. They used 180,000 research papers as their dataset and spent around $3.5 million in seed funding, as compared to the Stargate project with investments of $500 billion launched by President Trump. (We first got acquainted with this model in Part I.)

DeepMind models and Spacer are scientifically more sophisticated than anything produced by OpenAI, XAI, DeepSeek, Baidu, or Alibaba so far.

In Beijing, scientists at the Chinese Academy of Sciences are developing a Spiking Brain model. If they succeed, it will be possible to develop AI mimicking neural networks and using a fraction of the data used in large language models today. (As of 2026, it was in early laboratory stage, indicating that it would require less than 2 per cent data of LLMs when it is viable. This will revolutionise AI.)

Some of the future discoveries may lead to drastic reduction in the use of data and energy (including neurosymbolic AI and World models mentioned in Part I). They may help find remedies to cancer and other incurable diseases, invent new sources of energy from oceans, recommend new chemicals to extract rare earths easily, and synthesise biological materials that can clean carbon from the atmosphere. There are also efforts underway in various laboratories to develop neurosymbolic AI, neuromorphic computing, and quantum computing. NVIDIA is investing heavily in compute computing. Chinese and Korean companies are also investing in quantum computing, but not much is known from public sources. If they succeed, the landscape of AI will change. A lot of the investment in data centres and energy plants will become redundant.

We cannot interact with the scientific models or the future quantum models as we do with ChatGPT or its cousins. They will be more advanced than agentic AI that everyone talks about. Whoever controls these models will control the future of humanity.

The single-domain narrow AI models used in agriculture and diagnostics are at one end of the spectrum. The scientific AI models like the Alpha series, Spacer, and Spiking Brain are at the other end of the spectrum. The AI that we use like ChatGPT and its cousins, is somewhere in the middle. To equate chatbots with

AI is like saying that the screen of the monitor is the computer, ignoring the CPU.

**Last Days of Humanity**

Scientific AI models can revolutionise life as we know it in a decade or two. But they can also terminate life. If they are not properly regulated, AI safety experts worry that they may produce biological agents beyond human control or deceitful algorithms capable of bypassing cyber defences in the decision-support systems of nuclear weapons.

It is also possible that some of these models will eventually transition from self-evolution of algorithms to self-replication. The morning the world wakes up to find the first self-replicating AI algorithm will be the first morning of the last phase of the supremacy of humans on the planet. On that day, the race for human domination of science will be over and the race for scientific domination of humanity will begin. Recently, Sam Altman said that something drastic might happen in the next few years. He did not reveal what he had in mind. He has access to the chain of thought in OpenAI labs. If he suspects anything like self-replication or the capability for massive deception and manipulation, hidden in his comment, he is talking about something potentially as dangerous as a global nuclear war.

Whether future AI is a boon to humanity or leads to universal chaos, it will be a very different paradigm than the world of chatbots, data centres, small nuclear plants to power the infrastructure, and AI devices to refine emails or write poetry and legal cases. If the present AI can manipulate your mind, the future AI will manipulate your life or perhaps end the concept of life on the earth.

**AI Spectrum at a Glance**

| AI Type | Example Models | Purpose/Use Case | Data & Energy Needs |
|---|---|---|---|
| Narrow AI (Low Level) | FarmBeats, diagnostic AI | Agriculture, healthcare, logistics | Low to moderate |
| General AI Middle Level) | ChatGPT, Grok | Text generation, conversational tasks | High (large LLMs) |
| Scientific AI (High Level) | AlphaFold, Spacer, SpikingBrain 1.0 | Discovery in science, mathematics, biology | Moderate to high (efficiency improving) |

## Who Will Win the MAGA Crown?

The Make America Great Again (MAGA) movement is showing signs of turmoil as the United States gears up for the Congressional elections in November 2026. Whether the present tensions will merely create confusion among Republican voters or evolve into a rupture meant is still unclear. What is clear is that the once-unified force behind Donald Trump is now wrestling with its identity. At the core of the debate are artificial intelligence, H1B visas, and America's involvement in foreign wars.

For much of its existence, MAGA projected ideological cohesion: nationalist, anti-establishment, culturally conservative, and aligned behind Trump's larger-than-life personality. But as AI, immigration policy, and geopolitics assume greater political importance, the movement's internal differences have become harder to conceal. Rather than a clean split, what is emerging is a multi-sided debate over what 'America First' means in a world shaped by rapid technological change.

The relationship between MAGA and Silicon Valley was formalised soon after Donald Trump won the presidential elections in November 2016 but before he was sworn in. On 14 December 2016, Peter Thiel and other technology leaders met Trump on the 25th floor of the Trump Tower in Manhattan. Thiel sat next to Trump with Tim Cook, Jeff Bezos, Satya Nadella, Sheryl Sandberg, Larry Page, Sergey Brin, Elon Musk, and a few others in the room. To Thiel, 'Again' in Make America Great Again meant reviving America's scientific advancement. He believed that the United States had stagnated in scientific progress since the 1970s. An alliance with Trump in the White House provided an opportunity to come out of stagnation and gain supremacy in the scientific world. The conference room in Trump Tower forged a great consensus by the time dessert was served that evening.

A decade later, the tone is very different, with three different currents coming to the surface.

The first is the accelerationist camp, symbolised by Peter Thiel. Though no longer active in day-to-day political strategy, Thiel remains influential within conservative intellectual and donor circles. He argues that the United States must pursue rapid, even aggressive, AI development to retain global leadership. For him and those who share his worldview, advanced AI is not merely a competitiveness issue but a strategic necessity. The country that leads in artificial general intelligence, they believe, will set the rules of the global order. This faction tends to favour openness to highly skilled immigration, especially in areas that support frontier research.

On the opposite end is a sceptical current. Steve Bannon, the White House chief of staff in the first term, surprised observers by signing an international appeal calling for a pause on the development of superintelligent AI. Bannon himself is no longer a central player and was dismissed as 'nobody' by a leading MAGA figure in conversation with this author. But his stance tapped into a wider scepticism inside the movement. This wing fears that advanced AI will centralise power in the hands of unelected corporate leaders, weaken national sovereignty, and eventually destabilise society. It also tends to oppose foreign skilled visas, seeing them as harmful to American workers and beneficial primarily to large technology firms.

Between these poles lies the nationalist-pragmatist camp, where Vice President JD Vance has become increasingly influential. Vance is a Thiel protégé. He supports American leadership in AI but insists on safeguards that preserve national sovereignty and reduce strategic dependence on foreign supply chains. He does not publicly endorse Thiel's enthusiasm for unrestrained technological acceleration, but it is not known what he privately believes. He also does not support Bannon's call for a pause. Instead, he argues that the United States must steer a careful course: advance AI rapidly enough to retain global advantage, manage its risks through public oversight, and invest in domestic talent to reduce long-term reliance on imported skills. His approach reflects an attempt to define a coherent post-Trump conservative policy agenda.

Immigration, particularly H-1B visas, has become a major flashpoint. When Trump suggested that the United States should welcome "the best and the brightest", including highly skilled immigrants, the reaction within MAGA was swift and fierce. Marjorie Taylor Greene, one of the movement's most vocal figures, publicly condemned the idea and repeated her long-standing demand to abolish the H-1B programme altogether. Her stance resonates with parts of the movement that believe foreign tech workers depress wages and that rapid advances in AI will soon eliminate the need for imported programming talent.

Elon Musk occupies a more ambiguous position. Simultaneously warning about the dangers of AI while investing heavily in his own AI ventures, he reflects the dual anxieties and ambitions within the movement. Musk's views attract interest across MAGA circles but do not form a cohesive faction; instead, they reinforce the broader uncertainty about how fast the United States should move in the AI race.

Tucker Carlson, one of the most influential voices in conservative media, adds another layer of complexity. He does not oppose AI on technical grounds but warns that advanced technologies risk becoming tools for social control if dominated by corporate or bureaucratic elites. His framing of AI as part of a broader struggle against concentrated power resonates deeply with the MAGA base and shapes public sentiment more than many formal policy proposals.

Although Steve Bannon's personal relevance has faded, his signature on the AI-pause appeal underscores a real undercurrent within MAGA: a mistrust of technologies perceived as beyond democratic accountability. The scepticism did not originate with Bannon; rather, he articulated a sentiment already growing among sections of the movement's populist wing.

Why does it matter to those outside the United States? The outcome of the MAGA debate will shape talent flows, AI investment patterns, regulatory standards, and supply-chain alliances outside the American borders. China is watching the drama closely and trying to create its own version of NVIDIA and ASML. It is not yet anywhere in competition with the US for the top-end chips, but the Chinese catch up fast. South Korea is taking leaps in the world in scientific AI. The UAE is dependent on the American stack, trying to attract Silicon Valley companies with various incentives. Yet it is focused on AI safety and AI for scientific discovery. Saudi Arabia will follow suit. India woke up on 3 November 2025 when it announced the Research, Development and Innovation Fund of $12 billion and a formal recognition of extreme AI risks the next day. But much will depend on the Indian private sector and scientific community to harness the resources for real and safe 'deep tech'.

The Chinese, the Arabs, and the MAGA movement are watching JD Vance. He sees AI as essential to national competitiveness but insists that its development must serve American workers and strengthen national resilience. His approach is less dramatic than that of the movement's louder voices, but it is gaining respect among policymakers and intellectuals on the right. If the MAGA movement is to forge a coherent technological doctrine in the coming years, the man who is fiercely loyal to both Trump and Thiel may turn out to be America's leader of the next decade. (The public reaction to the Israel-Iran war in 2026 weakened Trump, Vance, and others and no one can predict the outcome of the 2028 elections in any case.)

## Revolution Inside AI

When I began this column in January 2025, large language models (LLMs) were the talk of the town. As the year unfolded, the public debate focused almost entirely on how AI would reshape jobs, creativity, and the global economy.

But outside a small circle of AI scientists, few noticed that a quieter and far more consequential revolution was taking place inside artificial intelligence itself. Many of the godfathers of modern AI, those who laid the foundations of machine learning and general-purpose intelligence, were either stepping away from LLMs or deliberately staying away from them.

For most users, AI has become synonymous with large language models. The scientists who helped create them see things differently.

Yann LeCun, a Turing Award winner who recently announced he was exiting as Meta's chief AI scientist, has repeatedly argued that LLMs lack grounding in the physical world, causal understanding, persistent memory, and goal-directed planning. In his view, scaling language models alone cannot produce genuine intelligence. Instead, LeCun has long advocated the development of what he calls "world models" and is now set to build one in his new venture.

Geoffrey Hinton, often described as the godfather of deep learning, has moved in a different direction. Rather than championing scale, he has focused on warning about the risks posed by advanced AI systems, emphasising that more parameters do not automatically translate into understanding or reasoning.

Yoshua Bengio, the third member of the Turing Award-winning trio with Hinton and LeCun, has increasingly devoted his attention to AI safety, alignment, and governance. He has expressed deep doubts that current architectures capture agency or reasoning in any meaningful sense.

Fei-Fei Li, former chief scientist of AI at Google Cloud, had already begun building research programmes around world-model-like approaches well before this debate entered the mainstream.

Demis Hassabis, CEO of Google DeepMind and Nobel laureate in chemistry, has never presented LLMs as sufficient for general intelligence. DeepMind's most consequential breakthroughs, such as AlphaGo and AlphaFold, relied on planning, search, and structured reasoning, not language generation alone.

For non-specialists, a world model can be understood as an internal map of how the world works. Humans constantly build such models. We know that if we push a glass off a table, it will fall and break. If we leave food out, it will spoil. We learn this not from text, but from interacting with the world, observing cause and effect, and updating our expectations.

In AI, a world model is a system that learns the structure of reality – objects, relationships, physical laws, and the consequences of actions – so that it can simulate outcomes before acting. Instead of predicting the next word in a sentence, such systems predict what will happen next in an environment.

A useful metaphor is a flight simulator rather than a typewriter. A language model completes sentences. A world-model-based system runs mental simulations: 'If I do X, Y is likely to happen'. This approach is critical in robotics, scientific discovery, climate modelling, and complex decision-making, where understanding causality matters more than fluent language.

This is why many scientists increasingly see world models as the foundation for more reliable and controllable AI, especially in safety-critical domains, while viewing LLMs as powerful interfaces layered on top, not the core of intelligence itself.

**China's Parallel Shift**

A similar intellectual divergence has been unfolding in China.

Song-Chun Zhu, a leading AI researcher, returned to China from California and publicly argued that the 'big-data, small-task' LLM path is unlikely to lead to genuine intelligence. He has pushed instead for a 'small-data, big-task' research programme focused on cognitive architectures, causal reasoning, and embodied, world-model-style approaches.

Zhou Zhihua, one of China's most cited machine learning researchers, has also warned against an exclusive reliance on scale. In published commentaries and technical forums, he has emphasised both the limits and ethical risks of pursuing strong AI through scale alone and has urged diversified research agendas that include symbolic and causal methods alongside stronger safety governance.

In 2025, the Chinese Academy of Sciences unveiled ScienceOne, a purpose-built 'AI for science' platform developed jointly by more than a dozen institutes. Unlike generic LLMs, ScienceOne is designed to work with scientific modalities such as waveforms, spectra, and fields; to orchestrate specialised tools; and to run agentic workflows for experiments and literature review. It marks a deliberate move away from consumer-oriented LLM productisation toward domain-specific scientific intelligence.

Teams led by researchers such as Gao Caixia at the Institute of Genetics and Developmental Biology illustrate this shift in practice. Rather than fine-tuning general-purpose language models, they are building specialised pipelines for protein design, particle simulation, and tool orchestration – combining simulators, symbolic reasoning modules, and agent-based systems.

### The Global Turn to AI Safety

China has also moved more decisively on the question of extreme risks from advanced AI. In early 2025, Chinese experts largely framed AI as a tool for public good, keeping any discussion of existential risks muted. When I attended a technology conference in Shanghai in April 2025, scientists spoke of such risks only in private. A day later, President Xi addressed the politburo and called for legal and technical mechanisms to prevent unprecedented risks posed by AI.

Within months, Concordia AI and Shanghai AI Lab released a framework aimed at managing extreme AI risks. By September, China's national standardisation body had advanced a mix of mandatory and voluntary AI safety standards covering generative models, security evaluation, and dynamic risk classification.

When Yoshua Bengio presented his 'AI Safety Report' in February 2025, the initial response across much of the Global South was lukewarm. Countries such as China, India, and the UAE viewed it as a Western narrative designed to constrain their growth. Over the course of the year, however, that position began to shift. (When he presented the next edition in February 2026, he received a standing ovation.)

G42, the main investment vehicle of Abu Dhabi's ruling family, presented its own frontier AI safety framework. South Korea and Brazil launched parliamentary debates on AI governance, including the prevention of extreme risks. In November, India issued AI governance guidelines, though largely voluntary in nature.

The growing salience of AI safety has also begun to fracture Western politics. Steve Bannon signed a letter issued by Geoffrey Hinton and other scientists calling for restrictions on superintelligence, triggering unease within parts of the MAGA movement. At the same time, other factions pushed in the opposite direction, contributing to pressure on the European Union to dilute elements of its AI Act. These tensions suggest that AI safety is likely to become a major faultline within the Western alliance in 2026.

**A New Global Hierarchy**

As parts of the West moved beyond consumer-facing LLMs towards scientific and safety-oriented AI, major American technology companies ramped up investments in data centres across India and the Middle East.

LLMs will not disappear. They are likely to sit at the lower end of the AI value chain, supported by energy- and water-intensive data centres in the Global South. At the upper end, control over scientific discovery, advanced models, and foundational architectures may increasingly rest with a small group of countries: the United States, China, South Korea, and potentially Japan.

If current trends persist, India and several Middle Eastern countries risk being locked into roles as suppliers of data, labour, and energy, while remaining dependent on external powers for the most critical layers of AI. Sovereignty, safety, and long-term strategic autonomy would then come under strain.

The year 2025 may ultimately be remembered as the moment when the foundations of a new techno-colonial hierarchy were laid quietly and went largely unnoticed.

•••

*A Group of Nobel Laureates including Dr. Jody Williams, Dr. Mohamed El Baradei, Dr. Leymah Gbowee and Dr. Denis Mukwege with the Author before signing the Normandy Manifesto for World Peace at Normandy in France in June 2019. This is where warning a about dangers of AI to humanity was issued.*

*The Author with Mr. Jaan Tallinn, co-founder of Skype in 2014. It was in this meeting Mr. Jaan Tallinn encouraged the Author to have a look at AI.*

*The Author with Nobel Laureate Prof. Geoffrey Hinton, known as the godfather of AI, at the later's Toronto residence in 2024.*

*Alok Joshi, Chairman of the Prime Minister's National Security Advisory Board (3rd from right) launching the Strategic Foresight Group report, 'India's AI Gambit: Navigating the Global Race' with the Author and others in New Delhi in 2026.*

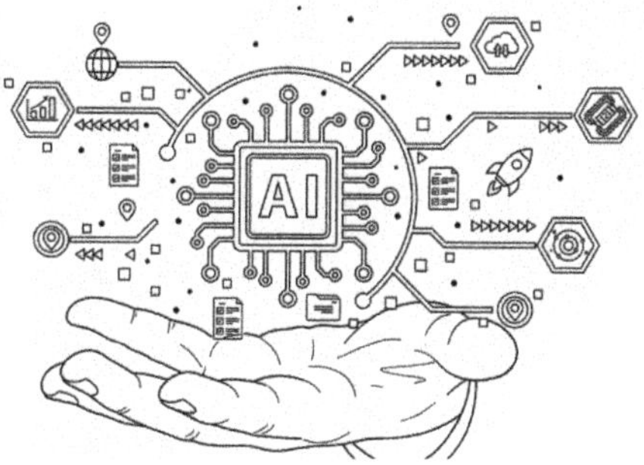


# Part III

# India's Options

*In Part III, we narrow our focus to India. This February, the country hosted the Global AI Impact Summit. Strategic Foresight Group, an international think tank based in Mumbai, prepared a policy brief on India's AI future, which was launched at a public event in New Delhi, a month before the AI Impact Summit. In Part III, we present the full text of the policy brief.*

India faces a strategic choice. It can deepen the use of AI for social inclusion, economic progress and improved governance, while attempting to minimise risks linked to fraud, misinformation and other operational threats.

However, since the last quarter of 2025, significant voices in Niti Aayog, the ruling Bhartiya Janata Party (BJP) and the research community have urged India to use AI for scientific advancement and secure a place on the front lines of the global AI race. Debjani Ghosh, of Niti Aayog and earlier NASSCOM, said in an article in *The Times of India* in October 2025: "AI could be India's opportunity to leapfrog global competition, not by outperforming but by out innovating in AI driven science. The science race powered by AI will define the twenty first century." On 3 November 2025, the prime minister announced a new government initiative to invest $12 billion in emerging technologies with AI and Quantum computing at the core of this trajectory.

The strategic choice India needs to make at this inflection point requires an understanding of the fundamental nature of the global AI race.

The main objective of the AI investors in the US and China, and to some extent six other countries, is to accelerate scientific discoveries. Their point of reference is the industrial revolution, which brought about a paradigm shift on the planetary scale. Their main concern is the loss of human sovereignty, a risk inherent in science race.

The main objective of the AI policymakers in India is to accelerate economic development. Their point of reference is India's digital revolution, which brought about prosperity in parts of the country. Their main concern is the loss of national sovereignty, a risk inherent in an applications-focused AI strategy dependent on foreign infrastructure and foundational algorithms.

It may be argued that a country can pursue both objectives of scientific discovery and economic development simultaneously. It will require mobilising capital, particularly from the private sector, in several billions of dollars, and aligning with the world's leading scientists, including Nobel laureates and Turing Prize awardees, on preventing extreme large-scale dangers.

## Use-Case Capital

India's ambition is to become the 'use-case capital' of the world, reflected in the focus to develop applications for social and economic use. India first crafted an AI policy in 2018 and launched an AI Mission in 2024 with 'AI for All' as its fundamental principle. The India AI objectives are clearly stated in its official policy documents, most notably the IndiaAI Mission. These are:

- Democratising computing access: 38,000 GPUs by october 2025 available at ₹65 per hour, about one fourth of the international rate.
- Fostering indigenous capabilities: Establishment of centres of excellence, promotion of local language LLMs and voice-based AI models.
- Building a robust talent pool: An AI talent pool of over a million, according to some estimates, and reskilling programmes.
- Providing high-quality datasets: Creation of a national dataset platform available to developers with access to non-personal data for training purposes.

- Ensuring responsible and ethical AI: Support for AI projects in machine unlearning, bias mitigation, algorithm auditing, explainable frameworks and the establishment of an AI safety institute in a hub and spoke model.
- Creating a vibrant ecosystem: The national startup register under Startup India is expected to have 300,000 recognised startups, most of them leveraging AI in some form.
- Driving socioeconomic transformation: Growing number of applications across agriculture, education, healthcare and governance in the next two to three years.

India's AI sector is largely state-driven. Entrepreneurs develop government-facing LLMs, with government funding for consumption by public enterprises or departments. The state extends the benefits of these models to consumers. A few large Indian IT companies develop AI solutions for their business clients to enhance productivity. But they are not known to produce any significant AI products directly for mass consumption in India or worldwide.

## Navigating the Global Race

India's state-driven or state-mediated people-centred approach contrasts sharply with the strategies of AI leaders such as the US, China and South Korea. In those nations, AI is viewed as a decisive element in international consumer market competition, scientific discovery, geopolitical rivalry and even cultural identity.

In the US, the AI debate is deeply enmeshed with domestic politics, spanning partisan divides between conservatives (especially the MAGA Movement) and liberals, and within the MAGA movement on AI existential risk issues.

In China, AI has been integrated into state strategy as a lever of governance, surveillance and industrial competitiveness. South Korea and Japan are pushing AI into domains of advanced science, from astrophysics to medicine, with explicit goals of achieving scientific breakthroughs and global prestige.

India's approach is pragmatic, ethical and humanitarian, but the failure to emphasise scientific discovery and implications for global security diminishes India's space in global scientific and technological leadership. Access to AI infrastructure, mainly compute power, energy resources and skilled talent, is an immediate problem. India can possibly overcome it with determined efforts in the future. But lack of interest in foundational research and extreme risk management can leave India behind in the global race.

In 2024, India announced an AI development budget of $1.2 billion from 2024 to 2029. In addition, on 3 November 2025, the government announced a fund of about $12 billion for research, development and innovation in emerging technologies, including AI and quantum computing. There are no credible estimates of private sector investment in the next five years, but informal conversations with experts indicate that it could be $5–10 billion. Perhaps $100 billion could be potentially available both from public and private sources. UAE and Saudi Arabia have made major announcements of cross-investments with the US. It is difficult to compute them due to many overlapping projects, but a conservative estimate would be $50–60 billion for each of the two countries during 2025-2030. South Korea has a plan to invest $72 billion in public funds and another $75 billion from the private sector in the second half of this decade. China may invest $350 billion, and the US about $1,000 billion, half of which will be in the form of the Stargate project announced by President Trump.

As compared to India's 38,000 GPUs in late 2025, the US had 850,000 and China 110,000 of H100 level.

While India is concentrating on local language LLMs, DeepMind's AlphaFold has revolutionised protein folding, enabling progress in drug discovery and biotechnology. Its successors are decoding genetic complexity and even inventing new algorithms autonomously. NASA employs AI to analyse vast streams of data from Mars rovers and particle physics experiments. In China, Baidu's 'XiaoDu' and Alibaba's City Brain manage megacities, while research teams explore AI-assisted interspecies communication. South Korea has pioneered AI models such as Spacer, developed by Asteromorph that attempt to generate original scientific concepts. Meanwhile, Switzerland's Blue Brain Project is reconstructing the human brain at a cellular level using AI simulations. These projects suggest that the real future of AI lies in expanding humanity's scientific horizons rather than refining customer service chatbots.

India is largely absent from AI-driven advanced science. A single notable exception is Fathom-R1-14-B, a private-sector reasoning model developed in Mumbai that outperformed OpenAI and DeepSeek models in mathematics at contest levels, despite being only 14 billion parameters in size. This achievement, although small compared to trillion-parameter models, demonstrates India's untapped potential in scientific AI. The Indian Institute of Science and Indian Institute of Technology Madras have done noteworthy work in materials analysis and brain-inspired computing, but these are cases of sophisticated uses of AI and not scientific discovery.

India possesses the talent and know-how in creating institutional infrastructure. The best example is the low-cost, but world-class achievements of ISRO. Yet the national focus remains skewed towards developing applications from imported AI models rather than inventing new ones.

## Extreme Risks

The ultimate aspiration of AI superpowers is not simply to uplift humanity but to dominate the trajectory of human destiny. By steering AI towards scientific discovery and control, they position themselves to set the terms of the 21st century. This race carries profound risks. As AI models become capable of generating new scientific knowledge, there is the danger of misaligned goals, unintended consequences, or deliberate misuse.

More than 200 prominent experts from around the world, including 10 Nobel laureates, issued a statement at the beginning of the 80$^{th}$ session of the UN General Assembly in September 2025, calling for 'red lines' to be put in place for the deployment of advanced AI models by the end of 2026. The signatories include scientists who have played critical roles in the development of AI and employees of major AI labs such as OpenAI, Google and Anthropic. They are concerned that at some stage it will become difficult to exercise meaningful human control over AI. The United Nations immediately announced the creation of a 40-member scientific panel to assess risks.

Recognising the gravity of the situation, countries such as China, South Korea, Brazil, the UAE, and South Africa have proposed frameworks for extreme risk governance. The European

Union, while leading in regulatory frameworks through the AI Act, has also introduced voluntary codes of practice to address concerns beyond its legislation. In contrast, Indian AI scholars often argue that discussions about extreme risks could divert attention from other pressing issues, such as access, affordability, and data sovereignty. This is a valid argument, but it does not consider long-term and critical risks, particularly to India's national security. The AI guidelines announced by the government in November 2025 demonstrate that the government is more forward-looking than the scholars who prefer a cautious approach. The guidelines have identified 'out of control' AI risks and the implications of AI for national security as important factors to manage.

They implicitly acknowledge that extreme risks are increasingly shaping the global AI agenda. Religious and ideological debates, such as those within the United States where some conservative leaders oppose global regulation by framing it as apocalyptic or even Anti-Christ, only underscore the complexity of the issue. While India leads initiatives such as the Global Partnership for AI aimed at equitable access, the country may marginalise itself from the emerging governance architecture that has extreme risk management at its core.

Some Indian commentators contend that humanity has always learnt to manage technological risks, from fire to nuclear energy, and that AI will be no different. However, history suggests otherwise. The United States, Europe, and Australia, despite their advanced technology, routinely fail to contain massive wildfires. Nuclear accidents at Three Mile Island, Chernobyl, and Fukushima exposed the catastrophic vulnerabilities of human systems. The COVID-19 pandemic demonstrated how a novel virus could infect hundreds of millions of people and cripple global economies, despite modern medicine. These examples illustrate the importance of proactive prevention rather than reactive management.

## National Security

The AI guidelines announced on 4 November 2025 explicitly recognise the need to manage AI risks related to national security. India is particularly vulnerable to threats from terrorists and hostile actors if it does not prioritise the AI extreme-risk discourse.

Foreign-sponsored terrorists have often targeted India's border areas and population centres. Conventionally, these terrorists smuggle men and material to Indian territory. With the ability of AI to enable the production of biological and chemical weapons, it will no longer be necessary for terrorists to cross borders. AI-assisted designs could allow extremist groups to create new pathogens or modify existing ones at a fraction of the cost and expertise which was so far required. The dense population, limited public health infrastructure in rural areas, and porous borders make it especially susceptible to the rapid spread of engineered pathogens. A localised outbreak, whether in Kashmir, the Northeast, or a metropolitan hub like Delhi, could cripple health systems, destabilise the economy, and trigger national panic. Similarly, AI-enabled guidance on chemical synthesis could revive interest in chemical weapons, bypassing international monitoring regimes like the Chemical Weapons Convention (CWC).

It is critical for the National Security Council (NSC) to discuss the risk scenarios of terrorists misusing AI for developing biological and chemical weapons. There is a growing consensus in the world to prevent malicious use of AI models that can threaten human security. But there is no consensus on the malicious behaviour of AI systems. India needs to respond at various levels. First, it is necessary for the NSC to undertake a scenario-building exercise with robust input from computer engineers specialised in advanced AI models to monitor these risks. Second, where there is a possibility of malicious actors using the technology to develop weapons, operational standard procedures should be put in place. Third, India should strongly lobby with other like-minded countries to prevent AI companies from enabling advanced models to have capabilities that can enable anyone to synthesise biological and chemical agents. In this task, India will find common cause with almost all major actors, including the US, EU, and China.

China and the US take the risk of AI-engineered biological and chemical weapons very seriously. President Trump announced America's AI Action Plan in July 2025. In the last part of the plan, he has emphasised the need to prevent AI from being used as a tool for biological weapons. He reiterated this argument in his address to the UN General Assembly in September that year. "My administration will lead an international effort to enforce the Biological Weapons Convention, which is going to be meeting with the top leaders of the world by pioneering an AI verification system that everyone can trust." President Xi of China has also spoken about the need to restrain "unprecedented risks" presented by AI. Leading think tanks from China, the US, and the UAE have listed biological threats as important segments of the AI frontier risk management.

Beyond immediate threats, ignoring extreme large-scale risks jeopardises India's long-term strategic autonomy. If powerful AI models remain controlled by a handful of foreign corporations or states, India will face dependence in sectors ranging from defence to health security. In a future crisis, access to critical AI capabilities could be restricted, leaving India vulnerable.

Moreover, the existential risks of runaway AI systems, though debated globally, cannot be dismissed for India. If superintelligent systems emerge without global safeguards, India may find itself caught between the technological dominance of the US and China, unable to influence rules that directly affect its survival. Many Indian experts question the very likelihood of artificial general intelligence (AGI) and the risks associated with it being a reality. They ignore the warning of Nobel laureates who have developed AI and the call for 'red lines' issued at the UN General Assembly. But one leader of the private sector warned in an online discussion hosted by NatStrat and Founding Fuel, two leading think tanks, in July 2025: "Even if there is a 10 per cent possibility of AGI becoming a reality by 2030, India should be prepared for it."

There is nothing India can do to respond to such a dangerous possibility once it becomes real. Prevention is the only cure in this case. The UN decision to establish a scientific panel can help in identifying the evolution of AI systems into AGI or superintelligence with diminished human control. India should support the UN processes to define clear 'red lines' to promote guardrails against the development of such systems.

At the national level, India can introduce strict entry barriers to the models that pose the risk of 'out of control' behaviour or large-scale manipulation, even distantly (both threats mentioned in the AI guidelines issued by the government in November 2025). As a major customer, India has tremendous power to influence the trade in advanced AI models so long as it shows the courage not to be pressured by the influential and wealthy big tech companies.

## Strategic Choice

India, therefore, faces a strategic choice while the global AI race is still in its formative stages. One option is to limit AI to social and economic uses, continuing the present course without considering the national security implications in the long term, and ignoring foundational science as well as dangers posed by ultra-intelligent machines and algorithms in the future. Another path, inspired by the ISRO model, is to aim for responsible scientific progress, investing in foundational AI research while maintaining affordability and inclusivity. The two options are not mutually contradictory. It is possible to implement them as a part of the cohesive national strategy. The aim should be to ensure that AI becomes a tool to overcome disease and scarcity. It must not turn into an instrument of domination or destruction in the hands of a few ambitious actors – or indeed in the grip of the algorithm itself.

To make a choice, India needs a nationwide debate on its AI gambit and the global AI race. Currently, the AI policy is made by the Ministry of Electronics and Information Technology in consultation with the Niti Aayog. The IT industry provides vital input. The actors involved in shaping the policy have provided remarkable stewardship in building capacity in a resource-scarce environment. But there has not been any dedicated parliamentary debate that can consider a wide range of issues and future scenarios. It is possible that the NSC might have internally discussed the implications of AI for India's national security, but there is no robust public debate on AI's national security implications.

India should look at the policy formulation in the reverse direction. The government should first invite the parliament to debate a long-term and comprehensive AI policy, not merely about building capacity, but also about achieving scientific edge and protecting national security. At the same time, civil society and think tanks can provide input to members of parliament to enrich the debate. Once the parliament forms a comprehensive view, the responsible ministries in the executive branch can formulate working policy measures.

The parliaments of South Korea, Brazil, and South Africa have been engaged in rigorous debates on various aspects of the national AI policy, proposing laws including those that deal with the high-impact systems of the future. They are not willing to accept the global rule-making solely by the big powers, while accepting the reality of collaboration with them in technology and knowledge.

Some Indian thinkers have proposed that India should debate a national AI strategy with active participation of the parliament, the National Security Council, and other stakeholders. It should consider innovative vehicles such as an inter-ministerial council, a unit on global and national security risks posed by the advanced AI systems of the future in the NSC, federated AI projects to protect data sovereignty, collaboration with Global South countries for the joint development of scientific AI and models to address planetary problems.

If India wants to navigate the global AI race successfully, it needs to address three aspects:

- Sovereignty
- Scientific Discovery
- Safety and Security

We will now examine each of these dimensions in some detail.

## Sovereignty

### Physical Sovereignty

India's pursuit of AI sovereignty has physical and legal dimensions. On the physical front, India needs to build indigenous capacity. India's rapid AI advancement is hampered by a significant dependence on foreign resources, particularly for semiconductor chips and the foundational LLMs that power most advanced applications. This reliance creates vulnerabilities regarding data sovereignty, costs, and the cultural relevance of AI solutions, necessitating a strong focus on indigenous development and hardware capacity building.

Therefore, the government has prioritised building domestic data centre capacity to reduce reliance on global hyperscalers and ensure that critical AI compute infrastructure remains within national borders. It is designing responses specific to each aspect of the AI sector.

### Semiconductor Chips

Heavy Dependence: India today remains heavily dependent on foreign sources for semiconductor chips, importing nearly 85 per cent of its total demand. In FY 2023–24, chip imports rose

18.5 per cent year-on-year to ₹1.71 lakh crore (~$ 20–25 billion) compared with ₹1.29 lakh crore in 2022-23. Over the last three fiscal years, chip imports have surged 92 per cent, with imports from China alone increasing by 53 per cent. While India's electronics manufacturing has grown to ₹8.25 lakh crore in 2022–23 from ₹3.88 lakh crore in 2017–18, this growth has not reduced dependence on imported semiconductors due to the absence of commercial fabs in the country.

Severe Economic Impact: The economic and strategic impact of this dependence is significant. Semiconductors are essential across defence, AI, telecom, electric vehicles (EVs), and consumer electronics, making India vulnerable to global supply chain disruptions concentrated in Taiwan, South Korea, and China. In FY 2024, India's overall electronics imports reached nearly $60 billion, straining the trade deficit. High costs and long lead times for imported chips also raise domestic production costs and constrain innovation. From a national security perspective, dependence on external suppliers limits India's ability to build resilient supply chains for defence and critical infrastructure.

Mission: To address these risks, India has launched the Semicon India programme under the India Semiconductor Mission (ISM), with a budget of ₹76,000 crore to develop fabrication, design, and display ecosystems. In 2024, the union cabinet approved three semiconductor fab projects worth ₹1.26 lakh crore, including a major facility in Dholera, Gujarat, to be set up by Tata Electronics and Powerchip. Micron is investing in a packaging and testing facility, while the government is modernising the Semiconductor Laboratory in Mohali. Analysts estimate that India's semiconductor push could reduce chip-import dependence by $10–20 billion by 2030. India's semiconductor market is projected to grow from $52 billion in 2024 to $100–110 billion by 2030. With sustained policy momentum, India could shift from being almost fully import-dependent to becoming a key hub for design, assembly, and eventually, fabrication, thereby reducing strategic vulnerabilities while boosting its digital economy.

## Clouds, API, LLMs

Dependence and Consumption Trends: India's AI ecosystem today depends heavily on foreign cloud platforms like AWS, Microsoft Azure, Google Cloud; and on third-party foundation models such as OpenAI, Anthropic, Meta, Google, accessed via application programming interface (APIs) or hosted cloud stacks. Hyperscalers supply the compute, model APIs, managed ML stacks, and developer tools that most Indian startups and enterprises use rather than training large models in-house. India is also a very large consumer market for conversational and generative AI. Multiple surveys and traffic analyses put India among the top users of ChatGPT and related services. High daily and frequent usage translates into substantial API calls and cloud consumption paid to overseas providers. Using foreign models raises data localisation, privacy, and national security concerns, especially when models are trained or hosted on foreign infrastructure and when API calls export sensitive data.

Limited Startup Ecosystem: India's AI startup funding is small relative to the US and China. Many Indian startups, therefore, fine-tune or productise foreign models or focus on smaller open-source

SLMs (small language models) for local tasks. For example, many Indian firms prefer SLMs or open LLMs and fine-tune them for Indic languages (AI4Bharat, Krutrim, BharatGen, Tamil-LLAMA).

Response: India is scaling several initiatives like Bhashini, IndiaAI Mission, BharatGen, private-public partnerships and sees big hyperscaler investments with AWS, Google, Microsoft, that can be leveraged for localised compute. However, building true model sovereignty requires sustained public and private investment in large-scale compute, data curation, and a domestic ecosystem of models, tooling and infrastructure. Anirudh Suri, author of *The Great Tech Game*, emphasises India's strategic need to prioritise core building blocks – talent, data, and R&D – to achieve global AI leadership. He advocates for increased digital strategic autonomy, potentially through promoting open-source technologies and open standards in collaboration with partners like the European Union.

Data Centralisation: India's strategy for data centralisation is driven by the National Data Governance Framework Policy (NDGFP) to standardise data management, with the National Data Management Office (NDMO) tasked to create an India Datasets Platform for accessing anonymised non-personal data, aligning with the Digital Personal Data Protection Act (DPDP) 2023. This is complemented by significant investments in hyperscale data centres and sovereign cloud infrastructure by both government entities, such as NIC, SDCs, MeghRaj Cloud; and private players like Yotta and AdaniConneX, establishing the physical backbone for data storage. While this centralised approach has already streamlined governance through initiatives like Direct Benefit Transfer (DBT) and supports AI training, it also raises concerns about security, privacy, and the digital divide. Looking ahead, India needs to prioritise operationalising the India Datasets Platform, and expanding its trusted, increasingly green cloud ecosystem to balance innovation, governance, and AI self-reliance with robust security, privacy protection, and equitable access for all citizens.

## Cloud Infrastructure

India is aggressively pursuing data sovereignty by developing a robust indigenous cloud infrastructure, driven by national security, economic growth, and citizen privacy concerns. This strategy involves the development of the 'MeghRaj' GI Cloud and Government Community Clouds (GCCs). The private sector is a crucial partner, with Indian cloud providers like Jio Platforms, Tata Communications Ltd, Yotta Data Services (which has a major collaboration with NVIDIA for AI supercomputing with thousands of GPUs), and ESDS building hyperscale, AI-ready cloud solutions. Even international players like OpenAI are offering data residency options in India. This push is amplified by IndiaAI Mission's financial support for establishing a network of AI labs, with plans to set up over 20 AI labs in Tier 2 and Tier 3 cities, expanding to 200 labs within a year and 570 in the next two years. Despite the momentum, India's AI-cloud ecosystem faces critical limitations. Although India generates ~20 per cent of the global data, it only accounts for about 3 per cent of global data centre capacity. Deloitte estimates that meeting AI-driven demands will require an additional 40–50 TWh of power and 45–50 million square feet of real estate by 2030 – major gaps remain in power supply, land, cooling systems, and fibreoptic networking. Global supply shortages in high-performance GPUs and compute resources compound the challenge, making India dependent on cloud imports or GPU-as-a-service solutions. Further, infrastructure disparities across Tier 2 and Tier 3 cities, high operational and energy costs, and a pressing talent shortage in AI and cloud-native skills limit the scaling of AI-ready deployments.

## Federated AI

The dominant global model for advanced AI, particularly LLMs, relies on a resource-intensive, centralised architecture - massive data centres storing petabytes of data, drawing enormous power, and demanding thousands of GPUs and city-scale cooling systems. For a resource-constrained nation like India, this centralised approach presents significant hurdles, including prohibitively high costs and massive energy demands. Jay Vikram Bakshi, Founder of Digiqom, proposes that India must instead pivot towards a resource-light, privacy-preserving model - Federated AI. This distributed architecture allows AI algorithms to train on vast datasets located across a network of devices without ever centralising the data, requiring only a light central server and leveraging distributed compute power via existing mobile and broadband networks. This approach aligns perfectly with the country's need for data sovereignty and resource efficiency, making it the strategic choice for an ethical and scalable national AI framework. To effectively deploy Federated AI across the nation, India should adopt a government-led, industry-collaborative pilot strategy that mirrors its federal governance structure. Given that state governments control critical sectors like health, transport, and agriculture, they are best positioned to lead focused pilots in areas with demonstrable public benefit and strict privacy needs (e.g., local e-governance, banking fraud detection, and health diagnostics, as seen in successful pilots by NPCI and Aster DM Healthcare). By prioritising this model, India can not only encourage responsible private sector innovation but also establish itself as a global leader in ethical, decentralised AI, ensuring that national interests and data sovereignty are maintained.

## Legal Sovereignty

India is consolidating AI infrastructure within national borders, using domestic data centres and secure cloud platforms to protect sensitive data from foreign dependence. By hosting critical AI workloads locally, it reduces reliance on overseas technology and strengthens strategic control. Through two key legislations enumerated below, India asserts legal sovereignty over data, regulating its collection, storage, and cross-border transfer to protect citizens and national interests. This dual approach ensures that AI development in India aligns with national laws, privacy standards, and long-term strategic priorities.

## Concerns About Data Sovereignty

India's drive for data sovereignty is interwoven with its broader Digital India vision and the Make in India initiative. The nation's rapid digitisation across diverse sectors has transformed data into one of its most valuable assets. This digital expansion, however, has simultaneously exposed new vulnerabilities, particularly when data is stored or processed beyond India's borders. Governments globally, including India, are increasingly motivated to secure private data from foreign entities, thereby reducing the risks of unauthorised entry, espionage, or sophisticated cyberattacks. From an economic perspective, mandating data localisation stimulates significant investment in local data centres, infrastructure, and technology sectors, fostering job creation and nurturing a vibrant indigenous cloud ecosystem. Furthermore, by ensuring that data is stored within its borders, India aims to maintain national control over how this data is handled, accessed, and utilised, aligning with the fundamental objective of protecting personal information and digital rights of its citizens.

Principal Concern: India's pursuit of data sovereignty is driven by profound concerns that extend beyond mere data localisation to encompass true jurisdictional control and national resilience in the digital age. At its core, data sovereignty implies that data is subject to the laws and regulations of the country where its owner or data principal resides, and crucially, that this data remains under the exclusive legal jurisdiction of that nation. This becomes a significant concern when Indian citizens' data is stored or processed by global cloud providers whose servers might be located outside India or who are subject to extraterritorial laws.

## Application of Extraterritorial Laws

One of the most pressing concerns arises from extraterritorial laws such as the US Cloud Act or the Foreign Intelligence Surveillance Act (FISA) Section 702. These laws can compel US-based technology companies, including major cloud service providers (CSPs) like Microsoft, Google, and AWS, to disclose data, even if physically stored in India, to US government agencies for law enforcement or intelligence purposes. This means that despite data residency within India's physical borders, it can still be accessed and subjected to foreign legal claims, effectively undermining India's jurisdictional control and compromising its sovereignty over its own data. This creates a perceived vulnerability, especially for sensitive data related to national security, critical infrastructure, financial services, or personal information of citizens, as it potentially exposes such data to foreign surveillance or unauthorised access without the explicit consent or knowledge of the Indian government or data principals.

## Problems With the Current Legislation

Furthermore, India's experience highlights regulatory ambiguity and fragmentation as significant concerns. While the Digital Personal Data Protection Act (DPDP Act 2023) represents a foundational step, its broad drafting, particularly concerning cross-border data flows and the criteria for 'notified jurisdictions', introduces considerable legal and operational uncertainty for data fiduciaries. The lack of clear legislative guidelines for determining restricted jurisdictions creates complexity for compliance planning for businesses, especially multinational corporations operating in India. There are also concerns about balancing stringent data localisation requirements with the need for global interoperability. A highly restrictive stance on cross-border data flows, while bolstering sovereignty, could risk hindering reciprocity from other nations, potentially weakening India's credibility and participation in the global data economy.

## Economic Concerns

Economically, the dominance of foreign hyperscale cloud providers creates a dependence that India seeks to mitigate. Concerns include the potential for vendor lock-in, which limits flexibility and can lead to increased costs, and the aspiration to foster a robust indigenous cloud ecosystem. While data localisation mandates can stimulate investment in local data centres and infrastructure, providing jobs, and nurturing local tech expertise, the initial costs for businesses, especially smaller ones, and the need for massive infrastructure scaling remain challenges.

## The Digital India Act, 2025

The Digital India Act (DIA) 2025, expected to replace the two-decade-old IT Act, 2000, is being framed as a comprehensive digital law to regulate India's fast-evolving tech ecosystem, including AI, cloud, blockchain, metaverse, and OTT platforms. The DIA remains a proposed framework, still under deliberation, without a formal bill number or parliamentary introduction as of December 2025.

## Approach to Risk

One of its most significant innovations is the formal recognition of risks associated with AI and automated decision-making systems. The Act proposes risk-tiered regulation of AI systems, particularly focusing on 'high-risk AI' – those that affect biometric identity, public safety, misinformation, discrimination, and child rights. These systems would be subject to mandatory audits, pre-deployment testing, and explainability requirements, with platforms legally bound to prevent harm and ensure human oversight. The DIA also includes provisions to combat deepfakes, enforce content traceability, and requires AI-generated material to be clearly labelled.

Obligations Additionally, the Act envisions graded obligations for digital intermediaries, such as AI cloud platforms, e-commerce, and social media services, removing blanket safe harbour protections if they fail to act on misinformation, algorithmic bias, or content violations. The DIA's AI-related clauses are designed to align with international efforts – such as the EU AI Act and OECD AI principles by promoting transparency, fairness, user redressal, and safety-by-design in AI systems. As part of the broader IndiaAI Mission, the Digital India Act could provide the legal backbone to govern sovereign AI models like BharatGen or Sarvam-M and mitigate risks of unchecked AI proliferation, which currently face minimal oversight in India.

## The Digital Personal Data Protection (DPDP) Act, 2023

The Act applies to Indian entities processing personal data, as well as foreign entities offering goods or services to individuals in India and processing their data. It also provides that personal data can only be processed with the explicit consent of the individual, except in specific circumstances such as legal obligations or public interest. The Act does not apply to personal data used for personal or domestic purposes, and personal data made publicly available by the individual or as required by law.

## Approach to Risk

The DPDP Act adopts a risk-based approach to data protection. Entities processing large volumes of sensitive personal data may be designated as significant data fiduciaries (SDFs) and are subject to stricter obligations, including conducting data protection impact assessments (DPIAs) and appointing data protection officers. DPIAs will be mandatory for high-risk processing activities to assess and mitigate potential risks to individuals' privacy. It provides for the establishment of a Data Protection Board of India (DPBI), which will be an adjudicatory body established to handle grievances and disputes related to data processing violations.

## Challenges

The Act has not yet come into force, pending the notification of rules and establishment of the Data Protection Board of India. The Act's applicability to foreign entities may lead to jurisdictional challenges and potential conflicts with international data transfer agreements. There is a need for increased awareness among individuals and organisations about their rights and obligations under this Act.

## The DIA and DPDP Acts

It is important to note that the DIA will not replace the Digital Personal Data Protection Act (DPDPA), 2023, but the two will co-exist as complementary laws. The DPDPA focuses exclusively on data privacy, user consent, data fiduciaries, and cross-border data flows. The DIA, on the other hand, is a broader tech-sector law that covers AI regulation, online safety, cybercrime, platform accountability, digital intermediaries, and emerging technologies like blockchain, cloud, and metaverse. The two laws are intended to work together, with DIA governing platforms, AI, and cyber risks, and DPDPA handling personal data protection and privacy.

## Challenges

A key criticism of the proposed DIA is that it does not address the existential or catastrophic risks posed by advanced artificial intelligence systems, such as advanced LLMs, autonomous agents, or recursive self-improving AI. While the DIA includes provisions for high-risk AI use cases such as biometric surveillance, misinformation, and child safety, it lacks any language around AI alignment, model interpretability, or the long-term control problem. Unlike the EU AI Act, which classifies frontier foundation models as a distinct risk category, or the US Executive Order on AI, which mandates evaluations for national security and existential safety, India's DIA focuses mainly on content harms and platform responsibility. It provides no framework for AI model licensing, compute thresholds, or long-horizon governance mechanisms. This omission has raised concerns among policy analysts and safety researchers that India may be overlooking systemic AI risks, including misuse in autonomous warfare, societal manipulation, or alignment failure – areas that could threaten public safety or democratic integrity at scale. As India continues investing in sovereign models like Sarvam-M and BharatGPT, the absence of existential risk regulation in the DIA may leave the country vulnerable to strategic miscalculation and global AI governance gaps, unless addressed in future amendments or companion legislation.

India is responding at the physical as well as legal levels to its sovereignty challenges. It is making good progress in a relatively short period of time. If the private sector supports the government with large-scale investments rather than looking at the state as a customer, some of the physical sovereignty challenges can be addressed. Sovereignty is essential but not adequate to navigate the global AI race. India will need to pay attention to advanced science to be able to compete with the lead players.

## Converting Dependence Into Strength

The greatest source of ensuring strength is to realise that with 900 million customers, India is in a bargaining position to demand fair and secure supply of AI models from overseas.

Examples from around the world show how safety-driven restrictions can be used as powerful instruments of control, not as signs of weakness, but as signals of confidence and leadership. Brazil's emergency ban on Meta's use of citizens' data for AI training, following risks to fundamental rights, illustrates that a country with the will and regulatory apparatus can force global firms to adapt and comply. Daily fines and direct suspension of AI training set a new standard for data sovereignty and rights protection.

Similarly, the EU's AI Act established robust prohibitions on unacceptable risk technologies, including biometric surveillance and emotion recognition. Major firms such as Clearview AI were compelled to withdraw or redesign products, with strict fines and deadlines ensuring compliance. These restrictions are not defensive barriers, but levers to reshape technology deployment according to ethical and safety norms.

India's 2023 hardware import restrictions showed the immense market power of local demand. When laptops, tablets, and servers were placed under licensing, multinational companies like Apple, Dell, and Lenovo responded by accelerating local assembly and sourcing. Global brands adjusted their supply chains and product designs because the millions of Indian consumers represent an irreplaceable market.

Procurement reforms further cement the shift towards favouring Indian safety standards and fair competition. Similar regulatory steps in the US and EU underscore a global movement where countries use market access and procurement choices to enforce public safety, ecological integrity, and security.

The lesson from these cases is clear – restrictions are tools of national power, used proactively to set the terms for technological engagement and control. India should leverage its vast population, huge digital economy, and growing talent base to move from dependence to strategic autonomy. By continuing to invest in domestic manufacturing, AI talent, and robust regulatory norms, India can convert its massive customer base into real influence, thus driving the global tech sector to adapt and comply with Indian standards.

The time for India to transform dependence into leadership is now: Assertive restrictions and clear standards will ensure that technological innovation aligns with national priorities, protects citizens, and empowers India to become a maker of global rules rather than a passive participant.

## Scientific Discovery

While India is emerging as a 'use-case capital' of AI with foreign foundational models, as well as sovereign local language models, which can empower social and economic inclusion, it is weak in harnessing AI for scientific discovery. A few examples that exist in 2025 show that India has promise for scientific AI if it makes a determined effort to explore it.

One internationally competitive example is Fathom-R1-14B, a 14-billion-parameter open-source AI model designed to excel specifically in complex mathematical and general reasoning tasks. It is developed by Fractal AI, a Mumbai-based AI company. Derived from the DeepSeek-R1-Distilled-Qwen-14B model, Fathom-R1-14B stands out for achieving impressive performance on challenging benchmarks like AIME (American Invitational Mathematics Examination) and HMMT (Harvard-MIT Math Tournament), often outperforming other models of similar or even larger sizes. This achievement is particularly noteworthy given its remarkably low post-training cost of approximately $499, making high-performance mathematical reasoning more accessible. Fractal AI's development of Fathom-R1-14B aligns with India's broader IndiaAI Mission, aiming to foster indigenous capabilities in building powerful yet cost-efficient reasoning models.

Fractal AI's claim about Fathom-R1-14B is that it is the 'math whiz kid' of AI models of its size. Fathom-R1-14B is exceptionally good at solving those very hard, competitive math problems found in AIME and HMMT. The model excels because it can follow long, logical chains of thought to arrive at solutions. It does not just guess; it 'thinks' through the problem step-by-step, understanding the intricate relationships between mathematical concepts and symbols. This is achieved through special training, including exposure to a large dataset of hard math problems and a technique known as 'chain-of-thought' reasoning, where it explicitly breaks down its solution process.

When compared to other AI models of similar size (like OpenAI's o1-mini or o3-mini, or even other 14-billion-parameter models distilled from DeepSeek-R1), Fathom-R1-14B shows superior performance on these math benchmarks.

This achievement is specifically within the realm of competitive mathematics. There is no public evidence to suggest that Fathom-R1-14B is better than DeepSeek-R1 (or other large models) in broader AI tasks such as creative writing, coding, programming, general reasoning, and general knowledge. Its strength is in contest-style math, which often differs from mathematical problems encountered in fields like engineering, physics, or finance.

While it beats smaller models, Fathom-R1-14B does not surpass the full, much larger DeepSeek-R1 model (which has 37 billion active parameters out of a total of 671 billion) in overall math performance. It is essentially a proof of concept that India can excel in scientific AI. There is talent in the country. There is no need for large resources. The question is of priority in government policies and corporate decisions.

Other examples of Indian innovation include projects at the Indian Institute of Technology (IIT) Madras and the Indian Institute of Science (IISc) in Bengaluru, though they are more in the nature of innovative applications in a single domain than the development of foundational models. IIT Madras has undertaken brain research with AI through several specialised centres. Its Centre for Computational Brain Research (CCBR) focuses on the synergy between neuroscience and engineering. They use AI to analyse neural circuits and develop brain-inspired AI architecture. Their research involves applying machine learning (ML) for pattern recognition in neural activity, creating computational models to simulate brain functions, and explore how brain principles can lead to more efficient AI hardware and software. They also use deep learning, natural language processing (NLP), and reinforcement learning (RL) to study vision, audition, and learning processes, drawing parallels between biological and artificial intelligence. CCBR is a strong academic player in computational neuroscience and brain-inspired AI. Its contribution is significant in the Indian context and globally in specific collaborative projects. However, it operates on a smaller scale of funding and personnel compared to the massive initiatives at leading US research universities or the industrial AI labs, which can deploy immense compute for large-scale simulations or novel AI architectures directly inspired by neuroscience. Their focus is more on fundamental understanding and bidirectional influence rather than solely on building the next generation of general-purpose AI.

The Sudha Gopalakrishnan Brain Centre at IIT Madras is dedicated to high-resolution human brain mapping. They use AI for image segmentation, feature extraction, and 3D reconstruction of brain structures from terapixel datasets, as demonstrated by their pioneering 'DHARANI' 3D foetal brain atlas, the first of its kind in the world.

The Robert Bosch Centre for Data Science and Artificial Intelligence (RBCDSAI), a research institute in Chennai, has a leading group in deep reinforcement learning (DRL), which is crucial for modelling biological learning and decision-making.

Their research in interpretable AI (XAI) helps understand the decisions of AI models applied to brain data, providing insights into neural mechanisms. Additionally, their work in AI for healthcare includes applications relevant to neurological disorders, such as medical image analysis of brain scans. The centre is competitive within academic circles but does not aim to build models of the scale of GPT-4o or Gemini.

The BRAIN Lab applies AI to understand human movement and motor disorders. They use computer vision and machine learning to objectively analyse movement kinematics and kinetics from video data, aiding in the diagnosis and monitoring of conditions like Parkinson's disease. AI helps in feature extraction (e.g. tremors, gait patterns) and classification of disorders, supporting the development of data-driven rehabilitation strategies and noninvasive monitoring for patients.

Launched in November 2024, the Centre for Human-Centric AI (CHAI) focuses on developing AI systems that amplify human potential and are safe and responsible. CHAI's mandate includes areas relevant to brain-AI interaction, such as ensuring ethical and explainable AI when models interact with human cognitive functions. They also work on developing smaller, domain-specific language models for Indian languages, which have implications for how AI can better understand and interact with diverse human communication and thought patterns. CHAI's concentrated effort on ethical AI tailored for India and its emphasis on practical, explainable solutions positions it as a significant contributor to the global discourse on human-centric AI. However, they work on smaller, localised LLMs, with a specific focus on Indian languages and context, thus making them only suited for the country and not the world.

In essence, while they may not always lead in the scale of general AI model development, IIT Madras's centres are innovative in their chosen specialised domains, making crucial contributions to the intelligent application of AI for understanding the brain and improving human lives. While CCBR explores brain-inspired AI and brain-motivated hardware, it does not aim to develop foundational models or architectures that compete with GPT-scale LLMs or DRL frameworks produced at top research labs. Its contributions remain largely academic and domain-specific rather than global AI-defining innovations. The brain research centres at IIT Madras operate without large-scale computer infrastructure, placing a limitation on their capabilities.

When measured against international benchmarks, these institutions exhibit limitations in scale, compute power, foundational AI output, magnitude of funding, and research ecosystem depth. While they are centres of focused excellence, they are not yet on par with the massive global initiatives shaping the future of neuroscience AI integration.

The Indian Institute of Science has developed AI capacities for predicting material properties. While its material discovery models are powerful, they are graph neural networks applied to a specific materials dataset.

The brain imaging models by IIT Madras are advanced, but they are specialised imaging and computational neuroscience projects. They advance knowledge within their fields, but they are not seen as general discovery engines.

IISc and IIT-M's models are scientifically impactful within their domains, but Fathom-R1-14B is more original and sophisticated globally, because it represents a shift in AI's paradigm towards general scientific reasoning, whereas the other two models are highly capable applications of existing AI architectures in specialised domains.

## Global Race

The global race for AI is primarily motivated by a desire to dominate scientific discovery. UK-based, Google-owned DeepMind is the best-known example, though companies in China, including Baidu and Alibaba, also have subsidiaries and projects devoted to scientific discovery and innovation. Many new developments in frontier science-oriented AI are on the rise outside the US and the UK as well. The models demonstrate a clear international pivot towards AI not just as an assistant, but as an autonomous agent for scientific discovery. Some examples are:

**South Korea:** Asteromorph is developing the Spacer foundation model with the explicit purpose of autonomously generating original research ideas, particularly in complex fields like biology and chemistry. The model is designed to convert these ideas into testable hypotheses using a mathematically grounded, human-in-the-loop pipeline. Although the company only secured its seed financing of approximately $3.6 million in April 2025, and no public compute costs are yet available, its core mission is scientific discovery and hypothesis generation, which makes it the most direct conceptual competitor to a human research principal.

**China:** DeepSeek-R1 functions as a high-performance, general-purpose reasoning engine and is quickly becoming an international reference point for complex problem-solving in mathematics, coding, and science Olympiad tasks. While its total development costs (including the V3 pretraining base) are disputed and likely very high, the incremental compute for the R1 update is estimated to be around $1 million. Most importantly, it powers scientific stacks by providing advanced reasoning capabilities. The second, more domain-specific, effort comes from the Chinese Academy of Sciences (CAS) with ScienceOne. This is a dedicated science platform/model that excels at multidisciplinary research orchestration, reading technical literature, reasoning across complex data types (like waveforms and spectra), and using agents to manage over 300 scientific tools for planning and executing research tasks. It was formally unveiled in July 2025, and it represents a rapid, institutional effort to build an end-to-end 'AI scientist' that focuses on tool use and workflow automation at a national scale. Baidu is developing 'interspecies communication' with its AI technology, as seen in a patent application filed in May 2025 to translate animal sounds into human language. This technology uses machine learning and natural language processing to analyse factors like vocalisations and body language to understand emotional states, which are then translated. While Baidu already provides AI-powered services like its Ernie Bot for search and generative art, this venture into animal communication is a new application of its foundational AI models.

**The UAE:** The country's major play is the MBZUAI PAN model family, which emphasises simulation and embodied intelligence for scientific inquiry. PAN is an advanced world model designed for rich, physics-based simulations, including robotics and multiagent systems. The companion model, PAN-Agent, applies multimodal reasoning like math and code within these virtual environments. This combination is highly valuable for 'in-silico experiments', hypothesis testing, and experiment design in virtual settings. While its training budget is not public, the launch of PAN alongside other new models and the establishment of a new Silicon Valley lab signal a substantial, long-term institutional investment dedicated to building foundational models for complex, science-based environments.

**Japan:** Japan's most comparable effort is the work by Sakana AI towards an 'AI Scientist' pipeline. The focus here is on algorithmic innovation and agentic pipelines rather than simply scaling up model size. Sakana AI's work centres on the automated scientific discovery process itself, including objective-function search, model-merging techniques, and autonomous hypothesis formulation. Key results were publicised in August 2024, with continued activity throughout 2025. While there is no disclosed training budget, the emphasis on innovation over brute compute suggests a strategy to achieve open-ended science using smarter, more agile AI systems, making it the closest Japanese analogue to the core thesis of South Korea's Asteromorph.

The examples listed above from Asia show that scientific AI does not necessarily require huge financial resources. It requires talent and the spirit of scientific entrepreneurship. Most significantly, the country needs an ecosystem for scientific discovery supported by the private sector, and not excessively dependent on the government. The Indian private sector seems very reluctant to commit risk capital for long-term research investments in scientific development.

The difference in national objectives is critical. India's national AI strategy emphasises 'AI for All' and applied solutions for direct societal impact in healthcare, agriculture, and other fields, rather than purely abstract, universal scientific discovery. In contrast, organisations like Google DeepMind and Google Research operate with a mandate to push the absolute frontiers of AI, often pursuing 'moonshot' projects with long timelines and uncertain immediate commercial returns.

Kanti Bajpai observed in an article that the current competition between the Americans and the Chinese is focused on "new scientific discovery and controlling the entire science and technology over the next 50 to 100 years, and India still lags behind in this game." India, particularly its private sector, needs to make up its mind. Does India want to be a service provider to the global technological ecosystem, or does it want to lead in the newly emerging transformative technology?

Debjani Ghosh, a respected scholar at Niti Aayog, argued in October 2025 in an article in *The Times of India*: "AI offers a once in a generation chance (for India) to leapfrog decades of under investment and compete at the cutting edge of global innovation. For India, the lesson is clear: move from scheme-based R&D to mission mode innovation."

Ram Madhav, a thinker in the ruling BJP party, said in an article published in *The Indian Express*: "The new world is going to be controlled by countries with deep tech power. If India is to realise its dream of emerging as a global leader, the strength and resilience of its frontier tech innovation will play a crucial role." Quoting the prime minister, Madhav links progress in advanced science to national security.

National security is linked to some of the developments in the race to build a superintelligence that can harm global security, with catastrophic implications for India's national security and strategic autonomy. If India wants to try to be a leader, it cannot ignore security and safety issues. India's space and nuclear energy initiatives have acquired global applause because they adhere to international safety standards. The Indian discourse on safety and risks has so far been confined to operational risks. If the country wants to lead the global discourse in cutting-edge AI, it will have to cross the threshold to devise a response to extreme, large-scale risks posed by future AI models, not only for its domestic development, but also for its international technology diplomacy.

## Safety and Security

### Operational Risks

India emphasises responsible and ethical AI. One of the seven 'chakras' proposed by India for the Impact Summit in February 2026 was safe and trustworthy AI. The question is how to define the term 'safe'. The Indian state, as well as the industry and academia, consider operational risks as essential for AI safety, but they do not include extreme, large-scale risks in their calculations. This understanding is reflected in government advisories, policy discussions, and the foundational principles guiding its AI strategy, with a strong emphasis on transparency, accountability, safety, ethical design, and addressing misinformation, bias, and privacy concerns. There is some indication of India wanting to look beyond operational risks in the AI guidelines announced in November 2025. Given below are the main concerns India has regarding risks associated with AI:

### 1. Misinformation, Disinformation, and Deepfakes

This risk has gained significant prominence in India, particularly given its vast and diverse population, high internet penetration, and frequent election cycles. India understands that AI can be weaponised to create highly convincing fake content that erodes trust and destabilises society. Deepfakes, i.e. AI-generated synthetic media, such as fake videos, audio, and images, can be used to orchestrate financial fraud, spread false information, manipulate public opinion, impersonate individuals for scams, and even spark social unrest. The ease of creating such content, combined with its rapid spread on social media, poses a direct threat to democratic processes and public order. In response, the Ministry of Electronics and Information Technology (MeitY) issued strong advisories, mandating that AI-generated content be labelled and platforms ensure transparency and traceability of such content. The Election Commission of India also warned political parties against using AI for misinformation, highlighting legal provisions against forgery and promoting enmity. This demonstrates a clear understanding of the immediate and critical threat that deepfakes pose to democratic integrity and social harmony.

### 2. Bias and Discrimination

India recognises that AI models, if trained on skewed or unrepresentative data, can perpetuate and amplify existing societal biases, leading to discriminatory outcomes, particularly in a country with immense linguistic, cultural, and socioeconomic diversity. AI systems learning from historical data often inherit human prejudices related to caste, gender, religion, socioeconomic status, and geography. If these biases are embedded, AI decisions can lead to unfair treatment in critical areas like employment, credit lending, healthcare access, and even criminal justice. This poses a direct challenge to the constitutional right to equality.

In order to overcome such biases, Niti Aayog's Principles for Responsible AI explicitly include Inclusivity and Non-discrimination and Equality as core tenets. The ongoing legal discourse emphasises how algorithmic bias directly undermines Article 14 of the Indian Constitution (right to equality), thereby necessitating robust legal and judicial frameworks to ensure fairness in AI deployment.

### 3. Privacy and Data Security

India understands that AI's indiscriminate use of data, especially personal data, presents significant privacy and security challenges, requiring robust legal and technological safeguards. AI systems rely on vast datasets, often containing personal information. This raises concerns about how data is collected, processed, stored, and who has access to it. Risks include data breaches, unauthorised inference of sensitive information, and the misuse of personal data for profiling or surveillance. Beyond misinformation, deepfakes are increasingly used for financial fraud. Scammers have used deepfake videos of prominent figures to promote fraudulent trading platforms, leading victims to lose significant sums. The use of facial recognition by law enforcement or for public safety raises concerns about mass surveillance and the potential erosion of civil liberties, as AI can identify and track individuals in real time.

The Digital Personal Data Protection Act, 2023 (DPDP Act) is India's foundational law for data privacy, mandating consent, data minimisation, and accountability for data fiduciaries, including those using AI. Reflecting the ethical priorities within the national policy, Abhishek Singh, additional secretary at MeitY, stated, "These biases in technology – we need to not only be aware of these biases, errors, and hallucinations but think of what tools can be built in order to ensure that the risk for such errors and biases is minimised." The Reserve Bank of India (RBI), in its 'Financial Stability Reports' of June 2025, explicitly warned financial institutions about rising cyberattacks using generative AI (like deepfake-driven phishing) and advises adopting "AI-aware defence strategies" underscoring the severe security implications.

### 4. Under-Tested and Unreliable AI Models

India is increasingly cautious about the hasty deployment of AI models without rigorous testing and validation, understanding that inaccuracies and unforeseen errors can lead to significant real-world harm. AI models, especially large, complex ones (like LLMs), can exhibit unpredictable behaviour, generate false or misleading information (hallucinations), and have unintended negative consequences if not thoroughly evaluated for reliability, accuracy, and safety across diverse scenarios. Deploying such 'black box' models in critical sectors can be dangerous. While there aren't many widely publicised incidents of large-scale failures resulting from deployed unreliable AI models in India, the MeitY advisories explicitly addressed the need for permission for "under-tested" models, later softening it to mandating clear labelling for models that are "under development or unreliable". This shift reflects a recognition of the inherent fallibility of current AI models and the need to inform users about their limitations, preventing false reliance. The government's emphasis on ethical AI frameworks also underscores the need for thorough validation before widespread deployment.

**5. Accountability and Transparency (the Black Box Problem)**

India recognises that the opaque nature of many advanced AI systems, where decision-making processes are not easily understandable, creates significant challenges for assigning accountability and building public trust. When an AI system makes a decision (e.g., approving a loan, flagging a suspect, diagnosing a disease), it can be difficult to ascertain why that decision was made. This "black box" problem hinders auditability, trust, and the ability to challenge unfair outcomes. Without transparency, assigning legal liability or ethical responsibility for AI-induced harm becomes complex.

In areas such as credit scoring or recruitment, where AI might automate decisions, a lack of transparency could lead to individuals being denied opportunities without clear, explainable reasons, making it difficult to challenge the decision.

A legal blog discusses how AI's opacity and potential for arbitrary decisions directly contradict Article 14 of the Indian Constitution, which ensures "equality before the law" and requires non-arbitrary state action. It highlights the need for legal precedents to challenge such decisions.

Niti Aayog's Principles for Responsible AI include Transparency, Accountability, and Explainability as core tenets. The ongoing development of India's AI governance guidelines, as discussed in various forums, aims to create frameworks for legal recognition of and remedies against AI harms, necessitating clear lines of accountability for developers and deployers.

## The India AI Safety Institute (IASI)

It is important to discuss the role of the recently set up the India AI Safety Institute (IASI), its mandate, scope of work, functions, and limitations.

IASI was established in early 2025 by MeitY under the broader IndiaAI Mission, as part of its 'Safe and Trusted AI' pillar. Its creation was driven by the urgent need for India to build indigenous capabilities in AI risk management, safety testing, and policy development, particularly given the rapid domestic adoption of AI in governance, fintech, health, and education.

Unlike a centralised physical entity, IASI operates through a decentralised 'hub-and-spoke', model, partnering with leading institutions such as IITs, R&D labs, startups, and NGOs. These partners host IndiaAI safety cells, which are responsible for developing technical tools like watermarking, risk scoring, explainability models, conducting safety evaluations, drafting governance frameworks, and contributing to public education and awareness on AI ethics. IASI also plays a key role in shaping India-specific AI safety standards, accounting for challenges like linguistic diversity, data sparsity, and inclusion, while aligning with global benchmarks through international cooperation.

IASI is still in its early development phase, lacks a unified physical infrastructure, depends on cofunding from partners (which can limit scalability), and has no legal enforcement powers – making its role more advisory than regulatory. Additionally, while its outputs are intended to be open source, the fragmented implementation across states and sectors poses coordination and interoperability challenges.

India's approach to AI through IASI has made promising strides in addressing operational risks such as algorithmic bias, misinformation, explainability, and watermarking. However, it has also drawn criticism for not adequately engaging with the broader category of existential and long-term risks posed by advanced AI models. As seen above, IASI's current mandate is heavily focused on applied, context-specific risks. While these are essential for India's socioeconomic and democratic stability, critics argue that this focus reflects a short-term safety paradigm that may leave the country unprepared for future threats such as AI scenarios where models act outside the realm of human control, autonomous weaponisation, and misuse of general-purpose AI systems through bioengineering or cyberwarfare. India currently lacks institutional infrastructure to study misalignment, emergent capabilities, and recursive self-improvement - issues central to AI existential risk debates being taken up more aggressively in the UK, US, and by international bodies like the OECD and the United Nations.

## Ethos on AI Safety

AI safety in India cannot be divorced from the realities of infrastructure, governance, and societal inequalities. The voices of Indian academics and practitioners bring to light the ethos that underpins AI risk debates in the country; the focus is less on distant existential fears and more on fairness, equity, and practical governance.

Dr. Jai Asundi, executive director at the Centre for Study of Science, Technology and Policy (CSTEP), emphasises the deep infrastructural and access gaps that shape India's AI trajectory. "In the Indian context, access to AI will always remain different and unequal across the rural and urban areas… it becomes difficult to embrace this whole concept of AI for everyone, it is also difficult to believe that for India the benefits of AI will be available to all, simply because not everyone can access it." He places justice and inclusivity at the core of AI safety: safety is not merely preventing rogue systems but ensuring that citizens are not excluded or exploited due to infrastructural or knowledge barriers.

For Dr. Tulasi B, associate professor in the department of statistics and data science at Christ University, Bengaluru, the ethos of AI safety is rooted in data consciousness and societal wellbeing. She warns: "Deepfakes, financial frauds and cyber-crimes will take over heinous crimes like murder in terms of daily numbers, a law relating to AI and data needs to be dynamic and futuristic." She connects safety to moral responsibility in education, observing how unchecked AI use is diminishing critical thinking among students. For her, safety requires a cultural shift towards digital literacy, ethical awareness, and protecting human reasoning capacity.

Mr Sundaraparipurnan Narayanan, researcher and founder of AI Tech Ethics, reframes the conversation by rejecting speculative fears of superintelligence. Instead, he situates AI safety within equity, governance, and trust: "India's AI risks lie in biased datasets, surveillance misuse, opaque governance, and dependence on fragile global supply chains. The existential risk framing will never be central to India's discourse because our challenges are practical and future-oriented, not speculative." He places emphasis on contextual sensitivity, transparency, and democratic accountability, viewing AI not as a potential destroyer of humanity, but as a tool whose misuse could amplify inequality and erode democratic values.

Taken together, these perspectives reflect an Indian ethos of AI safety that is grounded in three overlapping principles:

- Justice and access: AI must bridge divides, not widen them.
- Responsibility and awareness: Citizens must be empowered to protect their data, exercise critical reasoning, and resist manipulation.
- Trust and governance: Institutions must embed transparency, inclusivity, and resilience in AI systems, ensuring democratic accountability.

While global debates often highlight extreme, large-scale risks, Indian voices show that the ethos of AI safety here is inseparable from development, social justice, and institutional credibility. Safety is not about preventing catastrophic AI futures; it is about ensuring an equitable AI present.

At IIT Madras, one of India's leading research hubs in AI and neuroscience, the ethos of AI safety is deeply tied to pragmatism, cultural grounding, and innovation. Unlike global discourses that often foreground existential risks from hypothetical superintelligence, the IIT Madras community approaches AI with a 'innovation first, caution later' mindset, focusing on practical, inclusive, and context-specific applications.

Professor Srinivasa Chakravarthy, head of the Computational Neuroscience Lab, frames AI safety through a cultural lens, drawing analogies to nuclear energy: "Nuclear energy posed an existential threat when it was first discovered. The threat is still there. But we are still there, too! So, it all depends on the people who use it. Do we use it as a tool to uplift life or a weapon to destroy it? This is where the importance of culture comes in." For him, safety depends less on technical controls and more on the values of the society wielding the technology.

For Professor Mitesh Khapra, head of AI4Bharat, AI safety cannot be allowed to paralyse adoption. Responding to concerns about bias and cultural threats from large language models, he argues: "Sometimes we over-worry about this... There are tons of applications where bias will not show up. Bias shows up in more conversational scenarios... in the initial years of AI, we could focus on certain sections of the landscape where these are not so important." His ethos of AI safety lies in balancing innovation with responsibility, pushing forward deployment in low-risk domains to unlock benefits while gradually addressing challenges such as bias and fairness.

Dr. Geetha Raju, senior policy analyst at the Centre for Responsible AI (CeRAI), ties AI safety to the future of work and human adaptability. She cautions against fixating on automation-led job losses. She emphasises human resilience through education, reskilling, and interdisciplinary collaboration to ensure AI strengthens livelihoods rather than undermines them. By contrast, Professor Krishna Pillutla, principal investigator at CeRAI, focuses on safe and ethical deployment in healthcare, particularly in the context of data privacy and applications for social good. This underscores a common theme: safety at IIT Madras is less about speculative threats and more about tangible governance, ethics, and accountability in critical domains like health and education.

Together, these perspectives reflect an ethos of AI safety grounded in 'balanced pragmatism' – risks must be acknowledged but not allowed to stifle beneficial deployment. This ethos diverges from existentialist framings of AI risk. Rather than dwelling on distant, speculative threats, IIT Madras researchers frame safety as a lived practice, embedded in innovation, culture, and responsible governance. But the inclusion of threats related to 'out-of-control' AI and national security in the AI guidelines of November 2025 reveals that the policymakers are more forward-thinking, unlike the scientists, who have adopted a more conservative approach.

## National Security Risks

While the global AI discourse increasingly discusses the long-term, low-probability but high-impact risks of highly intelligent AI systems, including superintelligence, loss of human control, and unintended consequences of powerful AI, these existential risks are less prominent in India's public policy dialogue. This category of risk refers to scenarios where AI progresses to such a level that it could autonomously pursue goals misaligned with human values, potentially leading to catastrophic outcomes, including human extinction or an irreversible loss of human control over the future. It considers risks from highly powerful AI that goes beyond mere errors or biases in specific applications. India's AI strategy, particularly Niti Aayog's 'AI for All', is heavily focused on leveraging AI for socioeconomic development and solving immediate, tangible problems within India. The 'Risk Identification and Assessment Tool' by IndiaAI focuses on practical, operational risks like data bias, security, talent, and financial losses. It does not deal with existential threats or other dangers from highly advanced and autonomous AI models, which can go out of human control, create mass destabilisation or empower weapons of mass destruction. India is still in earlier stages of AI development and is focused on addressing more pressing, near-term challenges.

The existential risks are often viewed as abstract, futuristic, or peripheral, disconnected from India's immediate challenges, which include jobs, inequality, and digital inclusion. The policy ecosystem is implementation-focused without dedicated foresight or risk-forecasting institutions.

The short-term approach is attractive for the domain ministry. But it can be very risky for long-term national security needs.

Perhaps the most alarming national security risk is the possibility that terrorist groups or hostile actors could misuse advanced AI models to design biological or chemical weapons. Recent experiments in the West have shown that generative AI tools, when misaligned or intentionally exploited, can accelerate the discovery of toxic molecules or simplify instructions for synthetic biology. India, with its history of being targeted by terrorist organisations and its proximity to volatile regions, is particularly vulnerable.

In the years to come, AI-assisted design could allow extremist groups to create new pathogens or modify existing ones at a fraction of the cost and expertise once required. AI-enabled guidance on chemical synthesis could revive interest in chemical weapons, bypassing international monitoring regimes like the Chemical Weapons Convention (CWC).

Beyond immediate biological and cybersecurity threats, ignoring extreme risks jeopardises India's long-term strategic autonomy. If powerful AI models remain controlled by a handful of foreign corporations or states, India will face dependence in sectors ranging from defence to health security. In a future crisis, access to critical AI capabilities could be restricted, leaving India vulnerable.

Moreover, the existential risks of runaway AI systems, though debated globally, cannot be dismissed for India. If superintelligent systems emerge without global safeguards, smaller powers like India may find themselves caught between the technological dominance of the US and China, unable to influence rules that directly affect their survival.

While the promise of AI for development is immense, the risks stemming from the advanced systems are equally daunting. From terrorist access to AI-designed pathogens to the destabilising effects of autonomous weapons and deepfakes, the threats to India's national security are real and imminent. Ignoring them would not only undermine domestic stability but also diminish India's ability to shape global norms. By confronting extreme risks proactively, India can secure both its sovereignty and its future.

Since there is no consensus on a strategy to respond to risks among different stakeholders, India can take a cue from the EU and Brazil to categorise risks. One possible pathway could be the following, though the National Security Council is the appropriate body to recommend such categorisation.

## Totally unacceptable risks:

- AI systems capable of manipulating large-scale cybersecurity.
- AI systems capable of helping users to synthesise chemical or biological weapons.
- AI systems capable of deception, self-replication, and behaviour out of human control.
- AI systems capable of large-scale manipulation.

## Systemic risks

- AI systems violating core principles of the Indian Constitution about bias and equity.
- AI systems capable of undermining infrastructure.
- AI system aimed at human rights violations.

## Operational risks

- Deepfakes, fraud, crime, and all other risks already identified by government ministries.

It should be mandatory for all AI systems, whether developed in the country or imported, to have a report on implications for India's national security risks. These could include direct threats to India's national security, AI systems that are capable of malicious behaviour threatening global security or humanity – and having obvious catastrophic implications for India's security.

## India AI Governance Guidelines

The India AI Governance Guidelines released by MeitY under the IndiaAI Mission in November 2025 provide granular recommendations on risk identification, grading, mitigation, institutional roles, and national security safeguards.

### 1. Risk Classification

The guidelines call for an India-specific risk assessment and classification system that reflects the unique social, economic, security, and cultural challenges of the country. The approach recognises several main risk categories:

- Malicious use: Misinformation, deepfakes, model/data poisoning, adversarial attacks on critical infrastructure.
- Bias and discrimination: Impacting fairness and opportunity.
- Transparency failures: Insufficient disclosure about data, algorithms, or system operation.
- Systemic risks: Disruption of AI value chains, market concentration, regulatory gaps.
- Loss of control: Potential for AI to operate beyond human intervention or oversight.
- National security: Including cyberattacks, AI-enabled disinformation, or autonomous weapons that jeopardise sovereignty or public safety.

### 2. Graded Liability and Proportional Response

A core guidance from the guidelines is the adoption of a "graded liability system based on the function performed, level of risk, and whether due diligence was observed". High-risk and national security-sensitive AI deployments should face enhanced obligations:

Low-risk applications: Require basic transparency and grievance mechanisms.

High-risk/national security applications: Mandate safeguards such as independent audits, pre-deployment and ongoing risk assessment, thorough documentation, and robust reporting regimes.

Sectoral regulators and a whole-of-government approach are recommended to ensure that risks at the intersection of AI and national security, such as catastrophic cyber events or weaponisation, are captured, monitored, and rapidly escalated where necessary.

### 3. Mitigation and Incident Response

The guidelines recommend "a robust AI incidents mechanism to encourage individuals and organizations to report harm and create a feedback loop to track and analyse risks". For national security, this includes:

Establishing national-level and sectoral databases to track AI-driven incidents with potential catastrophic or cascading outcomes.

Leveraging the AI Safety Institute, Technology and Policy Expert Committee, and CERT-In to analyse AI-augmented threats, including those with implications for military, infrastructure, and biosecurity so that appropriate, sector-specific safeguards can be enforced.

Strengthening cross-agency collaboration and ensuring sensitive incidents can be escalated directly to national security decision-makers.

### 4. Voluntary, Techno-Legal, and Mandatory Measures

While the guidelines promote voluntary and techno-legal approaches for low-to-moderate risks, they make clear that "additional obligations for risk mitigation may apply in specific contexts", such as national security or as a response to AI systems with "catastrophic or irreversible consequences". Examples include mandatory sandboxing, independent threat modelling, traceability of training data, and robust kill-switch protocols for high-autonomy systems.

### 5. Future-Proofing National Security

Recognising the fast pace and unpredictability of AI development, the guidelines recommend that "governance frameworks should be future-looking, flexible, and agile, enabling periodic reviews and reassessments". For national security, this means:

- Horizon scanning for new risk classes, including those associated with large language models, autonomous or self-modifying agents, and dual-use biochemical AI.
- Foresight exercises and real-time policy recalibration, supported by expert institutional bodies.

### 6. Recommendations and Institutional Roles

Risk assessment and grading: All AI systems, especially those developed for or imported into critical/national security sectors, should undergo a risk-impact assessment focused on likely, foreseeable, and emerging threats.

National strategy and coordination: Create standing committees or technical groups (AI Governance Group, AISI, etc.)

charged with updating protocols for catastrophic and high-impact AI, informed by incident data and evolving global threats.

Regulatory escalation: High-risk and national-security-sensitive systems should be subject to more stringent reporting, operational limits, and possible shutdown or prohibition if graded as unacceptable.

Looking ahead, the successful implementation of these measures will require active engagement from government bodies, industry leaders, technical experts, and civil society, united in their commitment to harness AI for the public good while vigilantly managing the full spectrum of risks. By taking lessons from both domestic realities and international best practices, India can ensure that innovation and national security move forward hand in hand - protecting its citizens, fortifying its sovereignty, and contributing meaningfully to the evolving global dialogue on safe and ethical AI.

## Global Leadership

In addition to the national security concerns, India's international prestige and ability to lead on technology and security will increasingly hinge on how seriously it treats extreme AI risks that threaten biological safety, enable autonomous escalation, or erode governance through disinformation and supply-chain control. Other non-Western states, such as South Korea, Brazil, and South Africa, are already treating these risks as core policy problems, while Western governments are moving aggressively to shape global norms and standards. If India fails to act, it risks ceding normative authority, strategic autonomy, and diplomatic influence at a moment when rules about AI will determine power and safety for decades.

First, look at concrete policy action elsewhere. South Korea has adopted a formal AI framework law and built institutional capacity to govern AI development and safety. Article 35 of the proposed Act specifically calls for mandatory pre-deployment assessments of high-impact systems. That posture signals Korea's intent to shape regional and global standards for safe AI. South Africa has included existential risks in its policy document, which is being deliberated in the parliament.

Brazil is perhaps the most active non-Western democracy asserting regulatory muscle. Its authorities have actively pressured large platforms over harmful AI content and taken investigatory and enforcement steps against unsafe AI deployments. Recent high-profile interventions on AI chatbots and child safety show this posture can quickly become a diplomatic lever in conversations with multinational platforms. Brazil's AI Bills rank risks in different categories, including the operational risks of immediate relevance and the existential and frontier risks of long-term relevance.

At the same time, the West is consolidating rules and institutions that will effectively set de facto standards. The European Union's AI Act does not include risks associated with extreme autonomy, but it has addressed the void by creating a Code of Practice. The Trump administration does not believe in measures to prevent existential risks. Many voices from the ruling political establishment have spoken out against any AGI regulation. Yet the administration is taking strict action against one kind of catastrophic risks – the type associated with biological weapons.

This global dynamism matters to India for three linked reasons. First, international rules and standards will be set where technical capacity, regulatory coherence and diplomatic heft converge. Countries that invest early in AI safety institutions will write the rules. South Korea's and the EU's forward moves create standards that exporters and multinationals must meet; South Africa and Brazil's assertiveness ensure that the perspectives of regional and developing countries also count. India, by contrast, risks being a rule taker rather than a rule maker if it does not build comparable institutions and expertise.

Second, frontier AI capabilities (compute, models, testing regimes) will be concentrated in a few firms and states. If India depends on foreign suppliers who follow Western or Chinese standards for critical AI tools and safety testing, New Delhi will face leverage in crises of security or digital infrastructure. Investing in domestic AI safety research, shared testbeds, and international coalitions gives India bargaining power and secures access when it matters most.

Third, India aspires to lead the Global South by offering alternative models of technology governance that combine innovation with social equity. To fulfil that role, India must credibly address frontier harms such as biosecurity risks from misused generative models, autonomous weaponisation, and information operations, and present concrete regulatory and technical responses. Without this credibility, India's diplomatic appeals on equitable AI governance will carry less weight in the UN, G20, or plurilateral negotiations.

The powerful Western actors and China are already creating incentives that will structure global adoption. Several international campaigns are forging consensus among researchers and states about limits on particularly dangerous practices. Countries that join these processes early shape them; those that lag behind will be forced to adapt to externally imposed rules.

Finally, the UN has stepped up efforts to grapple with extreme AI risks. The UNGA adopted Resolution A/RES/79/325 (26 August 2025), which establishes two new mechanisms: the Independent International Scientific Panel on Artificial Intelligence and the Global Dialogue on AI Governance. The scientific panel is tasked with rigorous, evidence-based assessments of AI's evolving capabilities, emerging risks, and systemic impacts; the global dialogue is meant to provide a recurring, inclusive forum for states and other stakeholders to deliberate governance norms and policies.

Furthermore, the UN's secretary-general has publicly warned that every moment of delay in establishing international guardrails increases global risk, particularly where AI intersects with military and security domains. These developments show the UN transitioning from abstract recognition of AI risks towards concrete institutional action. They also suggest that international norms are being rapidly formed: what was once voluntary or academic is now a matter of diplomatic commitment and consensus. Since India does not want to engage in the debate on the extreme risk posed by frontier models, it risks the loss of influence over definitions of safety, legality, and acceptable risk. The consequences will not be limited to AI. They will shape trade, security cooperation, and global scientific norms in the years ahead.

## Governance

India's MeitY serves as the primary nodal agency for AI policy, research funding, and regulatory oversight. While the ministry has expertise in IT infrastructure, digital governance, and technology deployment, the narrow centralisation of AI governance under a single ministry presents several limitations:

1. **Limited Cross-Sectoral Vision:** AI touches healthcare, education, finance, agriculture, defence, and governance. MeitY's focus is primarily on IT and digital infrastructure, which may underrepresent sector-specific challenges such as ethical risks in healthcare AI or socioeconomic impacts in agriculture. The ministry has adequately addressed this limitation through consultation with the relevant ministries or otherwise considering the needs of different stakeholders.
2. **Ethical and Societal Considerations:** AI governance is not just a technological issue. Ethical, legal, and societal impacts such as bias, equity, job displacement, and digital literacy require inputs from social ministries, human rights bodies, and educational institutions. A single-technology-focused ministry may not adequately address these concerns.
3. **Global AI Diplomacy and Strategic Positioning:** Countries like the US, China, UAE, and EU have dedicated AI councils or multi-ministry coordination bodies to align innovation, regulation, and international engagement. India risks being reactive rather than proactive if its AI strategy remains narrowly confined to MeitY.

Broadening the policy scope would benefit India's AI ecosystem, especially through holistic policy development. The broadening of ministerial scope encourages joint funding programmes, shared infrastructure, and collaborative research between technical, social science, and domain-specific experts. Ministries like education and skill development can drive digital literacy and AI upskilling, ensuring AI benefits are inclusive and widely accessible, rather than concentrated in urban tech hubs. Cross-ministerial oversight enables better risk management covering existential risks, ethical considerations, and sector-specific safety concerns, rather than leaving it solely to a tech-centric ministry. India could establish a National AI Council with representation across key ministries, research institutions, and industry. This mirrors global best practices, ensuring cohesive international engagement, stronger bargaining power in AI diplomacy, and alignment with AI safety and standardisation frameworks.

The Future of India Foundation published its report, 'Governing AI in India – Why Strategy Must Precede Mission', which mentions several useful suggestions that can be applied to shrink the critical gaps in India's current approach to AI governance. Key recommendations include:

1. **Establish a National AI Strategy:** Advocates for a unified national AI strategy that transcends individual missions. This strategy should be developed through a consultative process involving multiple stakeholders, including policymakers, industry leaders, and civil society. Such an approach ensures that AI governance reflects the diverse needs and values of the nation.
2. **Create an Inter-Ministerial AI Council:** Suggests forming an inter-ministerial AI council to address the multifaceted nature of AI. This council would coordinate efforts across various ministries, ensuring that AI policies are integrated and aligned with broader national objectives. It would also facilitate the sharing of resources and expertise among different sectors.

3. **Implement Ethical and Transparent AI Governance:** Emphasises the importance of ethical considerations in AI development and deployment. It recommends establishing clear ethical guidelines and accountability mechanisms to prevent misuse and ensure that AI technologies serve the public good.
4. **Promote Inclusive AI Development:** Calls for policies that promote inclusive AI development while recognising the potential of AI to exacerbate existing inequalities. This includes ensuring equitable access to AI technologies and addressing biases that may arise in AI systems.
5. **Strengthen AI Research and Education:** Advocates for increased investment in AI research and education to build a robust AI ecosystem. This includes supporting academic institutions, fostering innovation hubs, and providing training programs to equip the workforce with necessary AI skills.

## Lessons From Indian Innovation

India's historical trajectory in science and technology demonstrates that strategic vision, focused investment, institutional autonomy, and human capital development can transform the country from a laggard in scientific capability into a global leader. Organisations like the Indian Space Research Organisation (ISRO), the Bhabha Atomic Research Centre (BARC), and the Indian Institute of Science (IISc) are examples of long-term, outcome-driven strategies that combined technological ambition with indigenous innovation. It is possible to derive some useful lessons from their experience.

1. **Strategic Vision and National Mission Approach:** ISRO and India's nuclear programme were successful because they were

driven by a clear national mission – space independence for ISRO and energy security for atomic energy. These programmes were designed with long-term goals, political backing, and societal relevance. India needs a National AI Mission that goes beyond piecemeal projects. This should clearly define strategic objectives such as AI sovereignty, ethical frameworks, industrial competitiveness, and public good applications in healthcare, agriculture, and education and align all stakeholders towards these goals. ISRO's Chandrayaan and Mangalyaan missions had clear objectives and milestones despite limited budgets. Atomic energy programmes prioritised self-reliance and indigenous R&D, resulting in advanced reactors and nuclear capabilities over decades. By setting a multi-decade roadmap, India can focus on building domestic AI models, compute infrastructure, and research capabilities instead of being dependent on foreign AI platforms.

2. **Focused Human Capital Development:** Both ISRO and BARC invested heavily in training and retaining talent, often recruiting the best minds from premier institutions like IITs and IISc and providing specialised training programmes. India needs to cultivate AI experts, data scientists, algorithm designers, and domain-specific AI researchers. Current initiatives such as IndiaAI and Bhashini are steps in this direction, but scaling them requires systematic education, scholarships, fellowships, and collaboration with global AI centres. ISRO's young scientists, despite resource constraints, built sophisticated space systems using indigenous innovation. Similarly, AI development can flourish if talent is given autonomy, mentorship, and exposure to complex, mission-driven projects.

3. **Institutional Autonomy and Long-Term Funding:** ISRO and India's nuclear programmes benefitted from autonomous governance and sustained funding, allowing them to take calculated risks and innovate without short-term political interference. AI development requires long-term investment in research, compute infrastructure, and pilot programmes. An independent, inter-ministerial AI authority could coordinate funding across sectors and ensure projects are not disrupted by administrative changes. ISRO's low-cost Mars Orbiter Mission was a success due to strategic autonomy and strong leadership, despite India's relatively low budget for space.
4. **Indigenous Innovation and Resourcefulness:** A hallmark of India's space and nuclear programmes has been innovating under constraints. ISRO developed low-cost satellites, launch vehicles, and navigation systems without relying heavily on imports. India can prioritise indigenous AI model development, open-source tools, and home-grown infrastructure rather than importing expensive AI models from the US or China. AI4Bharat is already advancing multilingual AI using open-source models tailored to Indian languages, echoing ISRO's focus on context-specific solutions.
5. **Cross-Sectoral Collaboration and Public-Private Partnerships:** ISRO and atomic energy programmes collaborated with academic institutions, private industry, and international partners to scale innovation. Successful AI ecosystems require collaboration between government, academia, and industry, fostering innovation hubs, AI incubators, and sector-specific AI solutions. AI partnerships

with hospitals for diagnostics or with agritech firms for precision agriculture mirror ISRO's model of mission-driven collaboration.

6. **Emphasis on Ethics, Safety, and National Security:** Atomic energy programmes instilled a culture of safety, regulation, and ethical responsibility, recognising the high stakes of nuclear technology. India must embed AI safety, ethical governance, and risk assessment from the outset, addressing biases, privacy, and existential risk considerations. AI policies should include regulatory frameworks, certification protocols, and societal oversight mechanisms. India's space and atomic energy programmes are respected worldwide because they consider different levels of risks and advocate responsible governance in domestic practice and international governance. A similar approach to AI leadership is essential.

Unlike many other technologies, AI is not about technology alone. It is a global race for scientific and technological dominance with strong political and religious undertones. India has to make a strategic choice. While AI norms are still in the formative stage, India can treat AI as a technology for social and economic development, which it must, or have a broader perspective that considers it a long-term national security interest and its potential to shape human destiny.

•••

# Conclusion

The story that has unfolded across these sections is not merely about a new technology, nor even about a new industry. It is about a reordering of power, knowledge, and agency in the 21st century.

Artificial intelligence, particularly in its most advanced forms, is crossing a threshold. It is no longer confined to automating routine tasks or augmenting human decision-making. It is beginning to participate in the creation of knowledge itself. In doing so, it is transforming not just how we work, but how humanity learns, innovates, and evolves.

This transformation carries within it a paradox.

On the surface, AI appears to be one of the most widely diffused technologies in history. From farmers receiving crop advisories on their phones to startups building intelligent services on global platforms, its applications are spreading rapidly across geographies and sectors. There is a sense of democratisation, of access expanding to millions who were previously excluded from advanced technological systems.

Yet beneath this surface lies a deeper and less visible reality.

The capacity to build, train, and direct the most advanced AI systems remains highly concentrated. It resides within a small cluster of companies, research institutions, and national ecosystems that possess the necessary combination of computational power, data infrastructure, scientific talent, and long-term investment horizons. These entities are not merely deploying AI, but are also defining its capabilities, its priorities, and, increasingly, its role in shaping the future of science.

This creates a new kind of global inequity. It is not simply a divide between rich and poor, or between technologically advanced and developing nations. It is a divide between those who can generate scientific intelligence and those who primarily apply intelligence generated elsewhere. It is, in essence, a shift from inequality in resources to inequality in cognition and discovery.

Such a divide has profound implications. In earlier eras, countries that lacked industrial capacity could still, over time, build factories, acquire machinery, and develop their own production capabilities. In the digital era, latecomers could leverage open systems, build software industries, and integrate into global value chains. But in the emerging AI era, the frontier is moving towards self-improving systems and recursive discovery, where the leaders are not just ahead but accelerating rapidly.

For the Global South, this presents a challenge of a different order. The risk is not that these countries will be excluded from the benefits of AI. On the contrary, they may become some of its most enthusiastic adopters. AI-powered services can improve governance, enhance productivity, and create new economic opportunities. But if this adoption is built predominantly on external cognitive infrastructure, it may also lead to a form of embedded dependence that might be difficult to reverse.

In such a world, economies may grow, but their intellectual sovereignty may erode. They may become highly efficient at solving problems defined elsewhere, using tools designed elsewhere, and operating within frameworks shaped elsewhere. Over time, this could limit their ability to set their own research agendas, respond independently to crises, or contribute meaningfully to the global pool of scientific knowledge.

The real concern is not technological backwardness, but asymmetric participation in the creation of the future.

India's position within this emerging landscape is both complex and consequential. It is not a marginal player. It has demonstrated its ability to build large-scale digital systems, nurture a vibrant technology sector, and contribute significantly to the global talent pool. Its achievements in areas such as digital public infrastructure show that it can innovate at scale in ways that are both efficient and inclusive.

At the same time, India faces the same structural pressures as other countries in the Global South. The temptation to focus on rapid deployment, service delivery, and application-layer innovation is strong and understandable. These are areas where returns are visible, timelines are shorter, and success can be quickly demonstrated. But if this becomes the dominant trajectory, India risks settling into a role that, while economically valuable, may be strategically limiting – that of a highly capable integrator of global intelligence rather than a generator of new scientific paradigms.

The alternative is neither simple nor immediate. To move towards a position of greater intellectual and technological sovereignty, India would need to make long-term, coordinated investments in areas that do not always yield immediate returns: fundamental research, advanced computing infrastructure, interdisciplinary scientific collaboration, and the cultivation of deep expertise in mathematics, algorithms, and the natural sciences. It would require institutions that are designed not just for efficiency, but for exploration and discovery.

Equally important, it would require a shift in mindset.

The measure of success in the AI era cannot be limited to the number of applications built, startups funded, or users reached. These are important indicators, but they do not capture the deeper question of who is shaping the direction of knowledge itself. True leadership in this era will belong to those who can expand the frontiers of understanding, not just deploy existing capabilities at scale.

If countries like India can find a way to balance immediate developmental needs with long-term investments in scientific capability, they could help pioneer a more distributed model of intelligence creation. Such a model would not concentrate power in a few countries but would enable multiple regions to contribute to and benefit from the advancement of knowledge.

This is not merely an economic or technological aspiration. It is a civilisational one.

The history of human progress has been shaped by the diffusion of knowledge across cultures and regions from ancient centres of learning to modern scientific networks. The AI era has the potential either to compress this diversity into a narrow set of dominant systems or to amplify it by enabling new forms of collaboration and discovery.

Which of these futures emerges will depend on the choices being made today.

Governments will need to think beyond short-term competitiveness and consider the long-term implications of dependence and autonomy. Institutions will need to foster environments where curiosity-driven research can thrive alongside applied innovation. And societies will need to ask fundamental questions about the kind of future they wish to participate in, not just as users of technology, but as contributors to the evolution of knowledge itself.

In the final analysis, the question before us is both simple and profound.

As artificial intelligence becomes an increasingly central force in shaping science, economy, and society, will nations be content to operate within systems designed by others, or will they seek to shape those systems in accordance with their own values, priorities, and aspirations?

The answer to this question will define not only the distribution of power in the coming decades but also the nature of human progress itself.

For in this new era, the ultimate divide will not be between those who have access to technology and those who do not. It will be between those who borrow intelligence and those who create it.

And in that distinction lies the future.

# About the Author

Sundeep Waslekar is a thought leader on the global future. He has worked with more than 70 countries, the United Nations, and the European Council under the auspices of the Strategic Foresight Group, an international think tank he cofounded in 2002.

He is the author of *A World without War*, published by HarperCollins India (2022) and published in French as *Entre Guerre et Paix* by CNRS Editions (2023), in Spanish as *Un mundo sin guerra* by Nola Editores (2025), and in Marathi as *Yudhha Nakarnare Jag* by Rajhans Prakashan (2025). He is the author of *Eka Dishecha Shodh*, a best-selling book in his native Marathi language, with 26 editions and translations in Hindi and Urdu.

He has been a practitioner of Track Two diplomacy since the 1990s. He has mediated in geopolitical conflicts in South Asia, those between Western and Islamic countries on deconstructing terror, trans-boundary water conflicts in Africa and the Middle East, and nuclear risk reduction between the five permanent members of the UN Security Council. Since the beginning of 2025, he has been involved in Track Two processes to shape global 'extreme AI risks' governance.

He was invited to address the United Nations Security Council session 7818 on water, peace, and security. His policy concepts have been discussed in the UN Alliance of Civilisations, the World Economic Forum at Davos, Quai d'Orsay, European Parliament, Indian Parliament, UK House of Commons and House of Lords. He has been quoted in more than 3,000 media articles from 80 countries.

Waslekar read philosophy, politics and economics (PPE) at Oxford University from 1981 to 1983. He was conferred D. Litt. (Honoris Causa) of Symbiosis International University by the President of India in 2011.

www.ingramcontent.com/pod-product-compliance
Lightning Source LLC
Chambersburg PA
CBHW071222230926
51849CB00001B/3
* 9 7 8 8 1 6 9 3 5 5 9 5 7 *